LITANY
AT NAZARETH

BY

Reverend James J. McNally

AUTHOR OF

MAKE WAY FOR MARY
ROCK OF TRUTH
UNTIL THE DAY DAWNS

New York
JOSEPH F. WAGNER, INC.
London: B. Herder

Nihil Obstat:

JOHN A. GOODWINE, J.C.D.

Censor librorum

Imprimatur:

✠ FRANCIS CARDINAL SPELLMAN, Ph.D.

Archbishop of New York

NEW YORK, JULY, 1958

(The *nihil obstat* and *imprimatur* are official declarations that a book or pamphlet is free of doctrinal or moral error. No implication is contained therein that those who have granted the *nihil obstat* and *imprimatur* agree with the contents, opinions or statements expressed.)

Preface

The title of this work is simple: *Litany at Nazareth*. The style of composition must appropriately be simple, for true love is an uncomplicated thing, and my purpose here is to aspire to increase love for God's own mother.

Primarily, but by no means exclusively, I have written this work for my fellow priests. It is of their calling to preach Mary from the pulpit, to speak of her in retreats, tridua, spiritual conferences, and to work for her through such organizations as the sodality. I have chosen to devote a chapter to each title of the Litany of the Blessed Virgin, and my plan is simple. In each chapter I have examined, certainly not exhaustively, one of Our Lady's perfections (in itself and in contrast with its opposing vice), then have applied what such examination has revealed to daily living, and finally I have gone to Mary in Nazareth in order to move from conviction to resolve.

Our religious nuns and brothers turn to contemplation of the virtues of Mary for strength in carrying out the duties of their heroic lives. Their meditations are no mere speculative exercises; they want to know Mary better in order to know her Son better, to grow from that better knowledge to a more intense love, in turn to serve more devotedly Him to whom they have dedicated their lives. For these also I have written.

The prayers of the author accompany his present aim that Mary may be loved even a little bit more than before.

THE AUTHOR

Contents

CONTENTS

CONTENTS

LITANY AT NAZARETH

Holy Mary

THERE ONCE WALKED THIS EARTH a woman of Nazareth, named Mary. Had we lived in those days and met her, we should have found ourselves in the presence of one who was immaculate. Mary was freed from original sin not merely at some time between conception and birth, as were John the Baptist and Jeremias the Prophet, but she was uniquely free from the precise moment of her own conception in the womb of her mother, St. Anne. For the first time in the history of mankind there emerged, when Mary was born, a creature graced always with absolutely no stain resulting from Adam's sin. It was a wonderful day for the world, one without precedent, when Mary came into the brightness of human living, for it marked the advent on earth of pure and complete holiness embodied in one of God's creatures.

Even for this reason alone—her Immaculate Conception—we address her in the litany as "Holy

Mary." No other creature can ever approach her holiness, an exclusive and appropriate gift from God the Father. Exclusive and appropriate, indeed, for from all eternity the Creator had ordained that she was to become mother of His Son.

Through all the years since Christ first came, Mary has been the soft reflection of heaven and its holiness, standing ever in the hearts of people as a tender, noble woman, so close to Jesus God as to challenge the imagination. Not only has she stood as this reflection, but Mary through the decades has walked in spirit among her people, bringing them the breath of God, consoling them in their grief, rejoicing with them in their gladness. "My delights were to be with the children of men," we read in the Book of Proverbs. Conversely the children of men have found their delights in being with Mary and, through that closeness, have found easier the road to holiness. Through her, too, some have discovered that path for the first time.

All of us have been created for everlasting holiness, the heaven of being with our God forever. Accordingly, there can be but one way to prepare for heaven properly, and that is to try sincerely for holiness upon this earth. It is a simple thing to be holy, and yet hard. It all depends on what we want the most. It depends upon whether we want to fulfill God's will or our own; upon whether we crave recognition for ourselves or for the God who made us; upon whether we desire worldly goods more passionately than we desire the surrounding presence of the living God. Holiness is simply that.

Naturally, because we are of the stock of Adam, we may fail at times. We may blunder, be unwise, do wrong. Basically however, to attain holiness, we need not dwell too long upon the evil we have done, but rather upon the reason why we do the wrong. We must repent sins of the past, but wisely we should be still more concerned about the reason for our sin.

We have to take at least some small time out, amid this demanding world of ours, and think of why we seem to want God and His holy will pushed aside while we fulfill our own. We must find out why we cry for appreciation and acclaim, while at the same time we are deaf to the words of the Psalmist who ceaselessly proclaims the majesty of the Almighty. We have to watch and see that the very things we live with—all our worldly goods—become not simply an attachment, but so much a passion that God's presence becomes to us rather blurred and indistinct.

Another fact we must remember is that we are bound to strive for holiness. This is an obligation resting upon each of us. It is not for us to choose another way. God made us to be holy. We might think of how the Church begins its salutations in the litany of Mary. It calls her "holy," and says, "Holy Mary, pray for us." Consequently, we who have been destined for eternal holiness, and who may find the effort burdensome in trying for holiness now, may just as well make up our minds that we must go to the Virgin Mary with no reservations and no holding back. She is the one immaculate. Though knowing what sin is and the dire results of it even in this life, Mary never had the touch of sin upon her, the only one in all of God's creation.

Mary is the Immaculate Conception. A hundred years ago she graced this world again with her presence. She came to Lourdes, in France, not once but many times, and during the intervening hundred years millions have gone to her for cures of body and an increase of faith. We who may perhaps be wandering away from our eternal goal because we want our way and will, because we want our reputation at the expense of God's, because we want our passions satisfied no matter whom we hurt, might well hurry to the side of Mary before it is too late. Ask her for a cure of soul and an increase in our faith. Ask her to reverse our way of thinking, so that now, while there is yet time, we may begin anew to tread the only path that leads to God, the one which Mary walked. Though we hear the same words which Mary once heard from Simeon, "Thy own soul a sword shall pierce," remember that sometimes we need the sword. Too bad it comes so late!

4

Holy Mother of God

MIRACULOUS, mysterious, wondrous it is to be the mother of the Son of God. This was Mary's remarkable privilege on earth and is her everlasting glory in heaven. She was a very young lady kneeling in devout prayer, pledging her virginity to God, when an archangel appeared. Gabriel gave his message and Mary bowed her head in humble acceptance. Instantly the world was different from what it had ever been before. The Son of God through the power of the Holy Spirit had begun His earthly living within the womb of her who is the Immaculate Conception.

Yes, the world was different from that instant and on. It had to be. God was on earth, though secluded within the sanctuary of Mary. During this period before His birth Mary must have lived as if she were in heaven. To reach out and touch the stars, to be warmed in the brilliance of the sun, mellowed by the softness of the moon would be as nothing to her whose frame encompassed now the Light of the World. Mary could see the universe in all its symmetry and bloom all about her, but He who is the source of all beauty rested so near to her heart.

Then came Bethlehem, when angels sang nearby and shepherds heard their voices and even found a star. Mary in a plain and humble place brought forth into the world her God, and our God too. Through the immaculate medium which was Mary, Jesus Christ came from heaven into our world for men and women to adore, and with whom little children would soon be able to play. Though her horizon was most limited and though she walked a land which is but a small portion of our globe, Mary had become the mother of the Son of God, and He would touch the heart of every one created, whether for acknowledgment or for disbelief.

Mother of God, how some of us forget that God as we grow older! Children of His very household, guided from our early days and cared for by our holy mother Church, how often have we wandered forth amid the lanes of twilight bliss and left interred in the grave of memory the Christ who comes to save us. We can leave Christ in many ways, in such foolhardy ways.

God is all and, in a way, we are but a trifle. Yet, well do we know that many times we have behaved as if we were the god, and Christ but simply tolerable. Christ is our God; yet how often have we tried to climb upon His throne and let our will be done instead of His, forgetting all the while that the only throne to which we should ever aspire is the throne of His holy cross!

Were we to keep in mind, day after day, the eminence of the Christ who assumed our humble nature, were we to ponder, every now and then, upon His infinite majesty, could we honestly take such delight in ourselves as we do? We may have added talents and ability, personality and power, with all our style and charm; but what are these to God who gave us all our gifts in the first place? More important, who enables us now to preserve these gifts? Why can He not take some of them away tonight? He might, and we could do nothing about it. Have we a certain hauteur because of our money and our possessions and the fleeting distinction they bring? Have we vanity because of good looks, a concealed enchantment at our own cleverness? One automobile accident could take these away in a moment. St. Paul, little giant of the past, has words to say concerning pride: "Let no one deceive himself. If any one of you thinks himself wise in this world, let him become a fool, that he may come to be wise. For the wisdom of this world is foolishness with God. For it is written, 'I will catch the wise in their craftiness.' And again: 'The Lord knows the thoughts of the wise, that they are empty.' Therefore let no one take pride in men."

Pride is a deceptive thing. It cancels all the good that we create. It shows an embarrassing love for self —unknowingly sometimes—and stifles love for others, even for God. Pride is forgery and fraud—the writing of our own signature on a check that belongs to God. It is born of the devil and deprives the Almighty of that which is due Him. Why lose the good which we perform in life? Why lessen the reward of heaven by searching for much commendation now? Is the comfort of Christ's praise not equal to the empty words of men? Perhaps it is time we saw Mary before we go too far astray.

It is not just a matter of a prayer to her now and then; rather it is a question of going to her home and being alone with her. Joseph will be away working, and Jesus probably about His Father's business. Watching Mary, listening to her counsel, conscious of the warmth of her presence, realizing her mother's understanding and her love, there would pass from our mind the inordinate regard we may have for ourselves, and from our heart would disappear that fondness we have for the deference of men. More, perhaps, even than this. She would remind us honestly that "He is the Lord our God . . . we shall not have strange gods before Him"—even the strange god of self.

Why not be told these words now by the mother of God rather than by Christ Himself on that day when it will be too late!

Holy Virgin of Virgins

ON THAT MEMORABLE DAY when the archangel Gabriel came down from heaven "to a town of Galilee called Nazareth," he entered the room of a virgin, "and the virgin's name was Mary." So writes St. Luke inspired. When Gabriel had delivered his message, Mary said to him: "How shall this happen, since I do not know man?"

Already years before, when Mary was only a little girl, she had promised to God a virgin's life, and on this occasion, in the presence of an archangel, she confirmed that pledge. Even though Mary learned from Gabriel that she could be the mother of Jesus, Son of God, even the startling prerogative of being mother of the world's Redeemer did not silence this question which revealed her love of virginity.

We know, of course, that Mary was exempt from the guilt of original sin and from its penalties as well. Nevertheless, when Mary, close to God as no other creature could ever be, should herself choose virginity as her particular state in life, she knew without conjecture that virginity is the gift beyond all others most desirable to God. And yet, in consenting to motherhood, she acknowledged that this state, too, is the gift next acceptable to God, though, to be truly a gift, motherhood must resemble the significance of virginity at least in its purity and continency.

Both of these estates are good—virginity and marriage. But each can be damaged, even destroyed. Virginity must be in the soul before it can be ever in the body. Our mind must mount the hill of God and reflect upon eternal truths, so much more real than things we see and hear and touch. Our will must be a generous one, strong and persevering. We must encourage our heart to be embraced by the wings of angels as much as by the overtures of men.

Virginity is a resplendent gift on the part of a creature to God. It means, at least in those things which are evident, a handing over of the sword, a surrender of carnal love, an attempt at channeling perfectly the affections of our human heart. The soul must aspire to the things of God, and in so great a manner that dedication of the body and its powers simply follows. It is not difficult to give our body back to God, and to prefer His divine caress to that of others, if—and only if—we first consecrate our

11

mind to Him, our will, our memory and our restless heart.

Virginity of body will not stand alone. It can be a cold and begrudging state, unless behind it burns a love of Jesus, unless there be a constant pursuit of His wishes and decrees. What kind of gift is virginity of body when a heart lacks charity or if one is proud? What sort of gift when one's mind is constantly on money and its amassment, when one will hurt his fellow man by words, and cut him deeply? Such virginity is like a flower, resting between pages of a book, lifeless and pale, serving only to contain memories of what was and might have been.

St. Paul, in the New Testament, exhorts the Thessalonians in almost the same breath to chastity and charity: "This is the will of God," he writes, "that you abstain from immorality; that every one of you learn how to possess his vessel in holiness and honor, not in the passion of lust . . . concerning brotherly charity there is no need for us to write to you, for you yourselves have learned from God to love one another. But we exhort you, brethren, to make even greater progress. Strive to live peacefully, minding your own affairs."

This same condition can affect those who are married, for the prime purpose of matrimony may become lost to view as time goes on, and pleasure for its own sake takes pampering sway. Continency and purity are then rejected.

Mary, our mother, is the virgin of virgins. Her soul was perfectly attuned to Christ, the Son of God. Though blessed with the prestige of her Immaculate Conception, she is, of herself, the perfect example of all that is so dear to the heart of Jesus in things of flesh. Compare ourselves with Mary, "virgin of all virgins blessed," virgin in body, but also and first in soul. Compare and regret! We, whose mind so often dwells on flesh, whose imagination is let run riot, should come near to Mary and see the strength of her who is the Immaculate Conception. Let us all look at her and know the fruitlessness of our own bodily passions illicitly satisfied. We shall know the futility of what we seek when we seek wrongly. We shall know our self-accusing heart.

Come to Mary and breathe the freshness of the dawn. Feel the sweep of clear fresh air about us. But we do not gain this through a single prayer. We have to stay with Mary and live her kind of life. It may seem too slow a life for some, too lacking in adventure. This is where we make our big mistake, for the most thrilling chase in all the world is the pursuit of God with Mary. It is so unusual to think this of a virgin. But she is "virgin of virgins" and can make us see things never seen before. She will take us from the caverns and the darkness and the valleys, where

13

we thought we were such sportsmen, and lift us high to the real field of life. Then, through Mary, we shall recognize her Jesus whom we should be hounding with our love, rather than the creature we may have been destroying with our lust.

Mother of Christ

WHAT AN AUGUST POSITION to hold in life: mother of Jesus Christ! What breathless joy for a woman to know. Castle first of God conceived, but not yet born; then, later, mother of a precious Son who left His mother's castle for a cave.

Before unearthly choirs filled the sky on a first Christmas night, Mary journeyed far and long to Elizabeth, her cousin, where her holy lips would form words everlasting: "My soul magnifies the Lord, and my spirit rejoices in God my Savior." Came the day a while after His birth, when Mary carried her infant Son to the temple in order to offer a sacrifice: "a pair of turtle doves or two young pigeons." In the joy of the occasion when this mother would be purified, Mary met the holy man named Simeon, ancient, wise and so desirous of holding close his Lord. Here was the first time that Mary heard harsh words, words that would foretell her future years, words that told her heart the awful price of being nearest, dearest to the Son of God: "Thy own soul a sword shall pierce." Then there was that day in the temple, years later, when Jesus, lost by His parents, told His mother that he must be about His Father's business. St. Luke says words that contain a universe of meaning: "his mother kept all these things carefully in her heart."

Yes, how carefully Mary must have kept them. How much she knew of Jesus! Through all her joyful, glorious days of living, and her sorrowful ones, too, the mind of that virgin mother was replete with things of God.

Are we not in a way, many of us, strangers to the Virgin Mother? Do we recognize her really as we ought? Do we pass her by and wait until another morrow to begin a life with her? Do we move only our lips in prayer to her, unmindful of the words we say, and thoughtless, inconsiderate about her dignity, her nearness to the heart of Christ? Are we moved by the joy she brings us when Jesus is a child, yet flee in the face of the piercing sorrow she feels when Jesus is a man? Do we welcome the cradle and not the cross, the garden of her house at Nazareth where Jesus used to play, but not the Garden of Olives where once He so generously prayed? Do we love to be near the Christ in a crib, yet fear to be near that Christ on a cross? Are we willing to accept Bethlehem because it is easy, but to flee the storm-

clouds of Calvary because it is hard? We think that
we are strong, courageous and valiant, and we go to
great lengths to prove it. Now look at our mother
Mary, never flinching from one of her trials; then
realize how much of our lives we spend in running
away!

Of course, on the other hand, countless souls are
living the life of Mary, and living it in close union
with her. They, too, tread the enchanted ground of
Bethlehem and Nazareth, but, when blight and trial
and burden come, they do not demur; nor are they
reluctant to walk the road to Calvary with Mary and
stand with her amid the thunder there. Numerous are
the men and women who know deeply what the cross
is like and who, to their glory, have accepted its
weight upon their shoulders and its ache upon their
hearts. They went to Mary in their woe, assured by
faith that she, who was the mother of Christ, would
certainly help when they were asked to share the
tears of Christ.

Innumerable are they who have been physically
healed at Lourdes and who have returned to their
lands and homes, restored, made whole; but much
more unnumbered are they who, visiting her shrine
in France, have, even though still lame, still blind,
felt the peace of heaven reach down and touch their
souls, bringing with it through Christ's mother a
burning charity, a hope astir, a faith reborn.

Mother of Christ! No union, no relationship could ever approximate the attachment which lived between Mary and her Son. No understanding can ever equal theirs; no hearts will ever be more allied. And, because of this, we who want so much to be good and to do Christ's will, might try to take an extra step toward Mary. No doubt we know her rather well in our days of joy and in our nights of pain. But we should take that further step.

Mary is the mother of Christ, and He it is whom we have been ordained to seek. Christ should be to us more real than any other person, whether it be mother, husband, child or friend. But it is difficult to reach beyond our limitations. We pray to Jesus, yet somehow cannot pray with him. We think of Christ, but somehow cannot think with Him. We love our Lord, but we cannot always love the things He loves, for we face a barrier—the barrier of people and things and places we may have to give up if we seek Jesus more realistically. Someone has to bring that barrier down. Who can remove it as easily as His mother! Why, then, be afraid of that one other step?

Mother of Divine Grace

IN THIS CREATED WORLD of ours we are all witnesses to beauty. We can stand on the terraced shores of carved lakes and see the token but suggested power of God's hand. We can go far up to the tops of hills and mountains to wonder at the masterpiece about us, formed by God's own fingers. We can dream on shores of great vast oceans and reflect upon the littleness of man compared to their roaring sweep and latitude. All of these but slightly mirror the Almighty and the imperishable beauty which He is.

We see beauty in the finely moulded feminine face, in the well-chiselled countenances of men. We see beauty in all style—of painting, phrasing, fashion, diction. We see it in the qualities of character—charity, generosity, heroism, long-suffering. Yet all of these are but a tiny image of the beauty that is God. From faith we know the beauty of a soul that has

God's own grace, and then our minds turn to Mary who is "mother of divine grace."

Mary did not have to wait for grace as we did by our baptism. From the instant when she was conceived, Mary was always in the state of grace. At Lourdes she told a little girl: "I am the Immaculate Conception." Then little Bernadette told all the world.

We are familiar with this exceptional position of Mary. As mother of Jesus who sends His grace into our souls principally through prayer and the sacraments, Mary is said to be "mother of divine grace." And being ever herself immaculate, she comprehends the miracle and mystery of sanctifying grace more so than does any other. Jesus merited all grace for us through His life, His passion and His death. Through all these stages His blessed mother lived with Him, united in a measure far beyond our own capacity for union. Mary gave Him love; she finished the cup of suffering with Him; and Calvary was the rapier thrust that pierced her soul all through.

Our constant aim in life, we know, is to be in the state of grace when we die, and our constant hope should be that we never lose that state before we die. Somehow or other, perhaps, we do lose grace. We let it slip from our possession because in the crisis we love ourselves more than we love Jesus. We inhale the capricious spirit of the world and follow its glimmering lights, forgetting that Jesus is "the way, and the truth, and the life." We seek self-praise and glorification and in the process, through our vanity and our pretensions, we push Jesus far into the background. We claim to our own credit the talents which we have, using them as if we were the source, not the benefactor. We do wish that we could forego sin, of course, and we want the state of grace, but the price seems sometimes high.

To regain what we have lost by sin, we need assistance. Again, to preserve the state of grace we still need help. And what more sustaining aid can we receive than that of Mary who is "mother of divine grace"? She knows the beauty of the soul adorned with God's great friendship, and the squalor of the soul without it. If we really want her to support us, then we must do more than say an occasional prayer to her. Our approach to her cannot be haphazard, nor can it be a solitary gesture now and then. We have to dwell with Mary and be with her in heart, morning, noon and night. It means living her kind of life, and that will take nerve, moral courage, and devotion.

Mary will clear up our thoughts concerning the state of grace, and we shall come to know that it is not simply freedom from mortal sin. That is the least of its elements. The mother of divine grace will teach us more and more that by sanctifying grace we share the very nature of God and, because God is a living Being, we share also His very life. At holy Mass, when the priest pours wine into the chalice with a drop of water, he prays, "O God, who has established the nature of man in wondrous dignity and even more wondrously has renewed it, grant that through the mystery of this water and wine, we may be made partakers of His divinity, who has deigned to become partaker of our humanity." In Christian marriage, for which we have such high regard, we can give to the one we love only what we have, not what we are. But God, when we are in the state of grace, gives us what He is.

What shall we do? Why not go to Mary's home, close the door behind us and tell her that we have come to stay? What a fascinating decision to make! To renounce the world's dim lights which unfortunately we may be seekin to discover a fresh sweetness in preferring love oi Mary to love of self; to fasten shut the windows of our soul, which are the senses, to temptation; to become master of our flesh instead of slave to it! Yes, a provocative decision to make! Are we willing? If not, why not? The answer we give may be the one factor that could send us to heaven.

Mother Most Pure

Mary is the Immaculate Conception. From the moment she was conceived in St. Anne's womb, Mary was preserved from the guilt of Adam's sin. God in His heaven had ordained that the future mother of His Son was to be exempt from the blot that has pursued all the children of Adam. God wanted her to be the perfect creature, but her perfection would not consist of being simply an ideal in a dream. Mary was not above the vicissitudes of ordinary living, and her perfection, in part, consisted of the fact that she was a woman of human flesh and blood, who bore the pains of frail humanity even more than we are asked to do.

Within the wide area of Mary's perfection we find her purity an ideal to which all men and women should aspire. She is termed "mother most pure," and is the mother of purity itself, inasmuch as she is mother of Jesus. Although exempt from the guilt of original sin and, properly speaking, not subject to its penalties, Mary nevertheless lived her life among the people of her time, enduring among her joys and glories the mental suffering and weariness, the distress, chagrin and shock that come to many mortals, but even then to a much more intense degree. One thing she need never suffer: temptation against the virtue of purity. God Almighty saw that His daughter was removed from that inclination. Yet in no way does this exemption from assault on purity in Mary's case give reason for us Christians to decry the comparison. On the contrary, Mary becomes the ideal we all would reach and, at the same time, the very human woman who, in bearing so many of the weaknesses of humanity, did not fail to undergo ache and anguish which would result from our own sins, especially those against purity.

All men and women, generally speaking, must struggle to be pure. Some are tempted more than others, and some unfortunately follow such temptations deliberately. We live with our fleshly bodies and, though God created them for a good purpose, we know that some often use it for evil. Since the fall of man in Eden, the flesh has become a formidable obstacle to serenity of conscience and to grace. It is present always, for good or for bad, and we must make the choice. St. Paul himself says to the

Romans: "I myself with my flesh serve the law of sin."

Because we are ceaselessly confronted with the appeals of our infirm flesh, we cannot afford to leave things to chance. To be victor over flesh we must plan a campaign against it; we must form our strategy with an eye to a long, drawn-out battle. The flesh is an able opponent, and it needs be conquered and subjected by design. Our plan should be of heaven and of earth. Purity of body naturally demands decency of mind and delicacy of heart. Consequently, if we would be sincere and honest in our effort to be pure, we must cast aside with firmness and alacrity the suggestive printed word, the obscene drawing, the loose and ribald conversation, the idle, wanton thoughts that seek a refuge in our mind. We should heed St. Paul who warned the Romans that "if you live according to the flesh you will die."

We need divine help, too, in this venture against flesh, and what is more obvious than that we seek it through Mary? Mary adds her intercession to ours. We cannot content ourselves with casual or incidental prayer if we would have her powerful intercession. We must approach her with earnestness and love. We must realize who she is, how pure she is, and what she will ask of us in return. Mary will ask us to be heedful of our eyes and what they like to dwell upon, of our lips and what they wish to feast upon, of our hands and what they wish to rest upon. She will ask us to visit Nazareth and remain with her. Evidently, then, there are some people whom we shall have to leave behind, and places to which we cannot repair again. How much are we willing to surrender in return for a life with Mary?

On the other hand, of course, we must not be unmindful of what Mary herself will offer us. Jesus knows; Joseph knows. To some a life in Mary's home might at first seem dull, confined and somewhat drab. No more would there be the scintillating and imaginative excitement of the evening which fades so quickly at the dawn. No more the passion of night with its sweat and remorse of the day. No more the sensual giant of illicit pleasure which becomes so coldly the maggot of desolation and of waste.

In exchange for the counterfeit of immoral pleasure, Mary would bring us the riches of true happiness and a tranquility of mind perhaps not felt before. She would teach us that beauty comes from within and goes far beyond the contour of the human frame. She would demonstrate that real joy is found more by far in touching the vibrant heart of God than in inflaming one of His beloved creatures. Mary would open to us a new world, one of light and love, respect and sometimes rapture. It is a world wherein we would be free, no more in bondage, a world that would contain a glimpse of heaven. With purity of heart and mind bred within us by Mary, we could step through the portal of this world and realize that, up until now, we perhaps have been even more foolish than the prodigal son of the Gospel, who had traded everything of value for the husks of swine.

Mother Most Chaste

THE HOLY FAMILY AT NAZARETH has always been
the ideal of Christian men and women. No
matter what our state in life may be, whether married
or single, mother, father, son or daughter, we have
always been able to focus our eyes distantly on far-
off Galilee, on Mary's home, and see there a perfect
model for our imitation and our guidance. The child
in a family was Jesus, Son of God, subject to His
parents. Single young men and women, attaining their
majority, also look to Jesus. Wives have Mary who,
in producing a Child, lost not her virginity. Hus-
bands have St. Joseph who gave to Mary not what
he possessed, but rather what he was.

Virtue was at home in Nazareth: humility and
charity, meekness, temperance and unwearied vigilance for the things of God, the Creator. Resplendent
among the rest was chastity, which made of Mary's
home an image of the house of God. Mary had been

conceived immaculate. No touch of imperfection reached her. She was the creature nearest God, a privilege reserved only for His mother. In her un-blemished womb once dwelt the unborn Savior. And Joseph knew, with the great grace he had received, that what was reserved for God was not to be dis-turbed by man. In the chain of happy service which bound Joseph and Mary to God, the link of perfect chastity was undoubtedly the strongest, for on the anvil in His heaven that link was forged by God the Father.

In our very practical, day-to-day world, God does not want us to avoid our duties and think all day and night of heaven. Nor obviously does He desire us so to labor now that we may find no time at all for thoughts of heaven. There has to be a happy me-dium, a blend of both our loves and obligations.

"Increase and multiply," said God Himself long ago, and that must always be our understanding in the case of human love. When a man and woman fall in love and marry, then the foremost purpose of their union must be to have children, to preserve and to conserve the human race, as God so ordered. For their willingness to help Him in His great work of creation, God has given to those who are married an anticipated reward of physical pleasure, as a certain compensation for the burden they will be expected to shoulder. To this bodily pleasure they have every right, as long as they observe God's decree.

We know from the lips of Jesus and from His teaching Church that no one has the right to seek sexual pleasure for itself alone, since this would be to convert the garden of love, where flowers bloom and grow, into a parched and arid land where nothing is sown but wildness. The single person is certainly barred from any intimacy of this kind with another, for the unmarried person is in no legitimate position to become a parent, and the pleasure is given by God solely for being willing to assume this function. We should take seriously the warning of St. Paul to the Galatians: "Walk in the Spirit, and you will not fulfill the lusts of the flesh. For the flesh lusts against the spirit, and the spirit against the flesh. Now the works of the flesh are manifest, which are immorality, uncleanness, licentiousness and such like. And concerning these I warn you . . . that they who do such things will not attain the kingdom of God."

The married person, too, who because of his state can lawfully join with God in the creation of a child, is bound by the virtue of chastity. He or she is obliged strictly to avoid any unnatural indulgence in sexual acts which are permitted to those married. Especially must birth control be shunned. Whenever sexual pleasure is secured by either married party or both, after precaution has been taken to avoid con-

ception, then does the virtue of chastity flee from
their hearts. This stolen pleasure results simply but
terribly in a pillage of the true love that binds lovers
in the sacred state of matrimony.

Let the married person also remember the words of
St. Paul to the Corinthians: "The body is not for immorality, but for the Lord. Do you not know that
your bodies are members of Christ? Shall I then take
the members of Christ and make them members of
a harlot? By no means! Or do you not know that he
who cleaves to a harlot, becomes one body with her?
Flee immorality. Every sin that a man commits is outside the body, but the immoral man sins against his
own body. Or do you not know that your members
are the temple of the Holy Spirit, who is in you,
whom you have from God, and that you are not your
own? For you have been bought at a great price.
Glorify God and bear him in your body."

Let those who search for earthly bliss within the
confines of the body, who wander paths dimly
lighted, confusing pleasure of the flesh with happiness—let them come out into the open where skies are
blue and consciences are gay. Let them come to
Nazareth in Galilee, to the virgin mother, Mary.
There will they soon discover the deception of which
they were victim, that they traded a birthright for a
mess of pottage. And Mary will take lurid memories

away, and she will lift the weight from their heart, the remorse from their mind. Mary will let them rest upon her shoulder, her arm about them—and they will never need another.

Mother Inviolate

AS WE REFLECT IN PRAYER and meditation upon
our Blessed Lady, our thoughts ascend to her
whose home is now above the stars, who, mother of
the Son of God, remains unchanged amid the un-
imaginable glories of heaven. We know that she also
is mindful of us as she listens to our every plea, and
hastens with them to the throne of God which she
knows so very well. She gives attention to the litany
of our petitions, and then brings them to the Heart of
Jesus, ever mindful that His will, not ours, be done.
Mary could hardly intercede in any other way.

Our Blessed Mother inherited all virtue. She was
immaculate, preserved from sin and all of its scars.
She had nobility, was upright, loyal and fair. Her integrity of life made it impossible that she would wish
anything contrary to her divine Son's will. Bethlehem brought its portion of hurt when "there was no
room for them in the inn." Later in the stable she

must have longed, perhaps momentarily, for the felicitation of her friends in preference to the uncomforting sound of sheep. Mary nevertheless accepted this deprivation not with resignation only, but also with a gladness and contentment because it was God's will. On the day of the presentation of Jesus in the temple, the aged prophet Simeon received the Christ Child into his arms and spoke of future travail to accompany the light and glory of the Messias. He spoke, too, of a sword to pierce Mary's soul because of the blind opposition that her divine Son would one day encounter. On Calvary the cup of her sorrow would indeed overflow in the cruel death of her beloved. And yet, no matter how bitter the prophecies and their fulfillment, no matter how keen the sword of sorrow, Mary's words in her Magnificat best show us the joyful obedience of her compliant heart: "My soul magnifies the Lord, and my spirit rejoices in God my Savior."

"Mother inviolate!" What a full understanding of what should be and what should not! What singleness of purpose made all her life a signal proof that God's will can be received with a holy resignation— even with desire! Sufficiently to comprehend this union of two wills, whereby Mary wished for nothing unless Jesus did—and for everything, including heartache and affliction, if He saw fit—is a step toward the knowledge that we ourselves cannot live apart from Mary in our lives, that just a random prayer is not enough to bring this closeness about. Such insight can come only from an ambition to take up our abode with her at Nazareth, to be with her when the sun brings its morning glow and the stars bring the reverie of evening.

Life has its trials and its conflicts. They are the lot of every one. And yet it takes us many years before we can with proper spirit willingly accept these crosses and these tears. We say in the Lord's Prayer, "Thy will be done"; but from long experience we know that in tribulation and in sorrow we sometimes mean little of what we say. That God's will shall be done is agreeable when things are going our way, but let the spectre of the cross come near us, and we scheme with all human ingenuity to drive the cross away. Oh, what we are missing, we who cry out, "Thy will be done," and do not really feel that way!

Crosses come to us because we are the children of Adam. They are as essential a part of our existence as are the smiles of fortune. God in His wisdom allows them to happen, for He knows that our gracious reception of the crosses He sends will form the image of Christ's own cross. When we have advanced this far, that we can easily perceive the resemblance between Christ's cross and our own afflictions and adversities, then are we indeed most blessed, for the grace of wisdom has been given us, and life

35

becomes that much easier and more understandable.

Ordinarily, we do not react this way. Days of prosperity we greet as if they were owed to us. Nights of loneliness, humiliation and of temporary failure we despise. Yet honestly, do we not deserve more by far a bitter draught? Let us look back at the past and see our offenses, whether of malice or even of weakness, and we shall see how much in atonement we owe the Christ who died for us. Would we, all alone, ever take up the burden of penance to make amends for our sins? Would we have the courage to request hardship and tears in apology to God for our transgressions of His law? Hardly, unless we are saints—and saints we are called to be.

Perhaps the time has come for us to realize that we shall never find happiness apart from God's will. The spirit of mammon offers us much, but always and only what is wanted by ourselves; it gratifies our desires; it satisfies our own self-will; it seeks to convince us that we are happy. We know that we can not possibly possess real happiness if we lose sight of God's holy will, so let us journey to Nazareth, with our minds made up to remain awhile. Mary will slowly review her own life, so intimately one with that of Jesus, and not merely because He was so closely associated with her as because she shared greatly in His cross. Mary will tell us that, despite her grief and sorrow, she was the happiest person alive, and she will tell us what she really meant when she once said to an archangel: "Behold the handmaid of the Lord; be it done to me according to thy word."

At first our stay with Mary may go much against the grain. Her simplicity of living and her singleness of mind would be so much in contrast to our complicated lives. But, as time goes by, we shall understand how Mary found such charm in life, why nothing except sin was ever counter to her will. If good things came she would rejoice; if heartache came, she perhaps rejoiced even more. There is the secret! Storm clouds or bright sunshine, it was the same to Mary. And so will it be for us, if we do not leave Mary. What a difference there will be between the inner joy of soul we possess in contrast to the selfish pleasure upon which we have spent so much time and with what futility!

Mother Undefiled

ONE OF THE PRINCIPAL REASONS—perhaps the most compelling—behind the Church's honor and regard for Mary, and behind the love which so many men and women have for her, is the fact that Mary never had to taste the dregs of sin's defilement. Mary came forth from the eternal cloister of God, fashioned untainted and unsullied, to live in a world which was witness to dereliction and error of every kind. She moved in these swamps of evil with soul pristine pure, just as it had been conceived by God, and with a heart that knew how properly to love and how to bestow affection generously and wisely.

When we think of Mary undefiled, we need not limit our impression to her purity alone. She was ever prompt to God's will in all things. Mary was diligent, large-hearted and had self-command; she was patient, deeply humble and liberal with her gifts from God. No vanity, perversity or self-indulgence; no scowls, no frowns, no hurt to others. No, Mary through God's grace was spared the residue of sin; she was spared even from the imperfections which the human heart usually fails to conquer. She is the masterpiece of God's creation, and in the Book Ecclesiasticus we read this tribute to her: "My spirit is sweet above honey, and my inheritance above honey and the honeycomb."

Every one of us, dwellers in this glade of tears, knows full well how imperfect we are. Try as we may to love God and to accomplish His will, we find ourselves faltering at every step of the way. We may go to confession often and renew our sorrow; we may receive the Body and Blood of Christ frequently, but, notwithstanding, we find the stain of Adam's failure pursuing us at every turn. We fret and chafe and are discontented. We utter words of which we are not proud a moment later. We laugh encouragingly at indecorous stories and sometimes even tell them. We find devious, though lawful ways, to circumvent the truth or offer pleasantries to friends, and we hypocritically withdraw them at home. Yes, we are filled with the vestiges of original sin so that our road to perfect love of God is hampered mightily. Strong temptation we may hit hard against and conquer, while yielding often to the little temptations. We may feel that, because we have eliminated grievous offenses from our life, we can ignore the slight ones, feeling somewhat that we can never do much about them anyway.

There is hardly one of us who does not wish that he could do better, who does not desire to love God more. Even they who sin seriously and continually, if possessed of strong faith—even they must wish that they could serve their God in a fine and holy way. So for all of us, whether we be frightful sinners or offend in just a minor way, it would be sensible to go to Mary, dwelling in her home at Nazareth. Perhaps it is not easy, naturally to make that journey even in spirit. There are so many things to do before we go, so much work to be accomplished, so many plans already made, but the value of our efforts toward perfection means setting all things else aside for a while at least.

Start gathering up the things which we may need for a visit to Nazareth. There should not be much to take with us. What really have we need for there? Little more than a heart which we must be willing to give her. There will be enough in Mary's house, even an abundance of things necessary. And Mary will greet us and make us welcome in words which the Book of Ecclesiasticus places on her lips: "Come over to me, all ye that desire me, and be filled with my fruits."

Yes, Mary has actually everything we want, but our pride of life and surging passions blind us to this fact. She has happiness and holiness and is our "mother undefiled." And is this not really what we want ourselves? Mary's love and understanding run quite deep, and if we were to remain there at Nazareth, she would help us so much in clearing our pathway to God.

From Mary we shall learn the need of loving God more than we do, and of using His creatures as He wants them used, not as we may have been accustomed to do. We shall learn that all our journeys into night for pleasure's sake do not bring happiness for long, but generally regret and shame. Mary would acquaint us with the fact that perhaps we are encumbered on the road to heaven with too many things, even too many people. The loudness of the world of men drowns out the voice of God, but at Nazareth the quiet voice of Mary would for a while shut out this clamor, and we should come to know ourselves much better. Do we really know ourselves now? We are defiled in many ways, beset with much concupiscence. We need to have the clear pure voice of Mary reaching our heart, so that we may be conscious of the distance we may have drifted from God in yielding to our lower nature. In the presence of Mary we shall see the greatness of our soul as God

41

created it and, as time goes by at Nazareth, we may even find it hard to leave her to return to the people and the things we once thought were the only factors which ever counted.

Mother Most Amiable

As we look through the pages of the New Testament and read the episodes wherein our Blessed Mother is mentioned, we note the recurring regularity with which Mary brought a feeling of happiness to those about her. Although overtones of sadness are perceived in each event, Mary's very sympathy and warmth enriched the hearts of others and brightened up their day.

In Bethlehem, when Jesus was born, Mary brought a holy joy to St. Joseph. It was to pervade all of his mystic life with Mary. And who can be unmindful of the fascination of shepherds on that first Christmas night as they were swept from dull and humdrum roles to stardom with Mary in a cave? Can we forget the temple in Jerusalem and the joy that flooded an old man's heart as Simeon took the Child from Mary and blessed God, saying, "Now thou dost dismiss thy servant, O Lord, according to thy word, in peace; because my eyes have seen thy salvation"? Behold the dramatic effect of Mary's visit to her cousin Elizabeth, when this elderly woman, barren for so long, but now six months with the child who was to be the Baptist, cried out, "The moment that the sound of thy greeting came to my ears, the babe in my womb leapt for joy." Incidentally, the Church teaches that at this moment he who was to be St. John the Baptist was cleansed from original sin. He was born, but not conceived, immaculate. When Mary and Joseph over a decade later had found their missing Boy, and Mary had spoken to Him in words which seem so much to be a reprimand, even then Mary brought happiness to the heart of her Son, for He was able for the first time to inform the world that He must be about His Father's business. At Cana in Galilee, Mary saved the situation for a bride and groom. And near the cross on Calvary the healing balm that soothed the broken heart of Christ was His mother. Yes, Mary inevitably brought happiness to others. How could she help doing so with her courteousness, her patience, her kindness and her love?

God created us for happiness on earth, a fact we must not lose sight of, no matter how frequently we are unhappy. As a result of original sin and our personal sins, our life is checkered with disappointment and with grief. We knew long ago that this would be so when God said to Adam: "Cursed be the ground because of you; in toil shall you eat of it all the days of your life." Nevertheless, God made us to be happy while we live, and our mistake consists in believing that crosses must necessarily take happiness away.

To a great extent our state of joy depends upon our fellow man. It is always in another's power to help or to hurt us, to send us the manna of cheer or the herbs of pain and vexation. While we are very conscious of all this, is it not at least possible that we forget we have this identical power of bringing smiles or tears to other human beings, and the obligation, too, of using that power for good? If God has created all of us for happiness on earth and if we can add to another's joy, then are we not bound to aid God in His purpose?

For many of us this takes much effort, yet the lack of kindheartedness is the reason for the melancholy of so many human hearts. It is hard continually to be kind to everyone, to those who displease or annoy us, to those particularly who lie, who cause humiliation, or who do us injustice. We feel like hurling at them all our vengeance. How can we be kind to them who have betrayed us? And yet, on reflection, are not all of these trials a slight image of Christ's cross, presenting us with the chance to share in it? We are often willing to bear any other cross except the one God wants us to carry. Notice how self-

willed we are, that we want even our crosses studded
with the ornaments of our own choosing! Have we
yet begun to look upon the unreasonableness of our
fellow man, his unfair criticism of us, his foul play
as providential opportunities for reducing the pun-
ishment due our sins, for lessening the penalty of
Purgatory? More than that, however! We should
experience a calmness of soul which far supersedes
the weary gratification of resentment if we accept
all these disturbances with equanimity. Bearing graciously within our heart the raw hurt of another's
thoughtlessness or malice will inevitably bring us to
more profound sympathy with the Man of Sorrows
and afford us a deeper insight of what He has done
for us.

It is rather difficult for us to accomplish this alone.
We need a model if we are to venture forth on this
new approach to our daily living. We need Mary,
for of all God's creatures she was the "most amiable."
Did Mary ever make a single person sad? She, too,
bore the brunt of conflict in her life, but never once
in all her trials did she bring disquiet to another. She
condemned neither the innkeeper at Bethlehem nor
the high priests on Calvary.

If we were to live at Nazareth for a time, it would
do our heart good. We should see her sweetness of
temper and be charmed at her gentle breeding at the
hand of God. We might even be confounded by her

patience, both the source and the result of her humility, and certainly we should be enchanted by her kindness and her love. Let us imitate her elegance and grace, and—who can tell?—we may help to convert a world by bringing to the saddened countenances of men the smile of God!

Mother Most Admirable

WE WHO HAVE BEEN GIFTED by God with our Catholic faith have never experienced difficulty in accepting the position of Mary in the Church. Others outside the pale of Catholicism have found the honor which we give her to be a lion in their path of understanding and forbearance. They expand on Mary's rare appearances in the New Testament, mentally whittle down her prestige, and fasten hard upon the incident in Scripture wherein Jesus, when He was informed of the presence of His mother and His brethren on the fringes of a crowd He was addressing, first said, "Who is my mother and who is my brethren?" Then, pointing to His disciples, He said, "Behold my mother and my brethren. For whoever does the will of my Father in heaven, he is my brother and sister and mother." Of course we know this to be in no way a denial of His blessed mother. Rather was it an encouraging statement that those who do the will of God are like His mother and truly are His adopted brothers.

No, we have never found Mary to be an obstacle to our faith in God. On the contrary, she has helped greatly in our understanding both of God and of the Church. She has made our faith alive; she has made sweet the diamond-hard words of the Church's doctrines; she has given strength to all of us in accepting, keeping and even loving the moral law. For them who feel sometimes to be far away from God, Mary has reduced the distance; for those who feel already close, she has placed their hands upon the heart of Christ.

The virgin mother is the ideal to us all, but a very practical ideal. We have placed her upon a predella, high above the rank and file, but she is a woman who never hesitates to come down from that pedestal to walk among the children of men. We are in admiration at her unique place in human history. We are in wonderment when we picture her with Jesus for so many years, learning from Him directly so many of heaven's secrets, giving Him, on her part, the glory to which human nature can ascend. And we are forever grateful to the living God that He has allowed Mary to be enshrined in our hearts.

With Mary ever in view as an object of admiration, we might do more than simply pray to her. Of course, prayer is tremendously important and is not lacking on the lips of our people. But we might try to imitate her more. It is easy to be like Mary, yet so easy to be unlike her. There is a certain grossness in our nature as a result of Adam's fall which constantly tempts us to give vent to the baser things of life. At times we hear deep within us the vibration of man's first rebellion in the Garden of Eden, and to that echo of waywardness we sometimes reply, yearning to cast aside, as did Eve and Adam, the gift and grace of God's own life for the devastating fascination of forbidden fruit. We feel as Lucifer felt when he said, as narrated by Isaias the prophet, "I will ascend into heaven, I will exalt my throne above the stars of God; . . . I will be like the Most High." Our own self-will is what we really wish glorified, and Satan will help us along by saying to us, as he said to Eve, "God knows that when you eat of it, your eyes will be opened; and you will be like God, knowing good and evil." The catastrophe could happen to us as it happened to Adam and Eve.

When we yield to the lower elements of our human nature, it is primarily our own will we want satisfied, no matter in what form or shape. The gratification of our self-will is the basis of sin. We become angry, because our will is opposed; a man divorces a woman, or a wife a husband, because either's way of life is restrained; this is why revenge is sought, why we hate our enemies, why we refuse the poor, why we judge others unfairly. This is the similarity we have with fallen angels and archangels: the common cry, "We will not serve."

Run to Mary, we who feel that we may fall from grace. Seek the haven of her house where we shall be safe from the rovings of the tempter. Until the day we die we shall be harassed and pursued by him, for, as St. Peter says, he is always "seeking someone to devour." Place ourselves in Mary's home, where Eden for a while can be forgotten, and look upon this second Eve who has helped replace the debacle of Paradise. Place our hand in hers, and notice how quickly at this union the serpent will slink away.

Placing our hand in that of Mary's may mean the relinquishing of some things we hold dear. It demands more than prayer alone; it requires the voluntary rejection of what may cause conflict in our soul, the things we have so long desired, so long possessed. It calls for the hard decision to abandon our own will and to break off with the pride, the pleasures and resentments which we have been coddling day after day. How could we be so close to Mary and continue to nurse the very things which make her sad? Nazareth with Mary might startlingly bring to light one certain sin that dominates our life, causes all our loss of grace and which we least expected to discover. We think we know our sins at present. True, we may have knowledge of what they are, but not, most likely, why they are.

Mary is our "mother most admirable." She entertains all virtue. We claim loudly that we love her. But stay for a while with her at home and find out why we do not love her enough.

Mother of Good Counsel

ONE OF THE MOST CONSOLING titles of the Blessed Virgin Mary is that of "mother of good counsel," because, to a large degree, it is that gift of the Holy Spirit of which most of us stand much in need, a gift which many of us reject or ignore.

We learn a great deal of Mary's good counsel from her silence in the New Testament. Certainly for many years she lived a life in Nazareth which was normal for that day and age. Later on, when Jesus began His public life and storm clouds of impending passion began to gather in the Judæan sky, Mary became the confidante of chosen Apostles, intimate friend of the many who followed her Son's every word and deed, and the comforting ally of her neighbors. Perhaps Mary needed help in those times more than they, but we cannot imagine this daughter of the eternal Father seeking strength from any human source, seeking comfort from any one but her God.

In the climactic days of Christ's last year, when leaders of His people were determined He must die, Mary it was of all the rest who stood out calmly against the brewing turmoil and who made tranquil the terror that ran wild through human breasts. The New Testament records a paucity of her language, but this in no way means that Mary had but little consolation and advice to offer. Rather does it signify how greatly her presence alone sufficed as her good counsel in place of many words.

The New Testament is primarily the story of Jesus Christ, His life, His passion and death. Under the persuasive promptings of the Holy Spirit the Gospel writers have concentrated completely on this portrayal, introducing Mary only on occasion, seemingly, too, only when she served to bring into clearer focus the Son of God Himself. But that she was a conventional woman, meeting her neighbors and speaking with them through the day, as women customarily do, should not be overlooked or forgotten. Only her dramatic words are mentioned in the Scriptures, but we can assuredly surmise that often in her personal conversations Mary was lending her good counsel.

We should be presumptuous if we claimed no need of Mary's counsel because, no matter who we are or what we are, the road to God is rather hard to walk alone. There are many enemies along the way. Our flesh with its recurring turbulence, the spirit of the world with its pretense and masquerade, the restless and alarming breath of Satan—all these will set their ambuscade and trap us when we least expect it. Though we are familiar, of course, with these enemies of our soul, we are not always very intimately acquainted with the way in which these enemies operate. We suddenly become affrighted at the fact of our own sins, but, at the same time, we are not very conscious of the reason why. We may be opinionated and quite impatient with another; perhaps we harbor grudges and are hypercritical. Even to the poor we sometimes show just a heart of stone, unmindful of these words of Jesus: "What man is there among you, who, if his son asks him for a loaf, will hand him a stone?" Although no stranger to our sins, we may be unable to detect what basic power of our lower nature has erupted into causing them. What real motive was there lying underneath?

There is hardly a doubt of our own wish to live sincerely, to live unfeignedly with God and with our fellow man. We wish that we may be good always, in love with Christ, and Him in love with us. But suddenly we face temptation and slip more swiftly into sin, and again we find ourselves no longer friends with Jesus. Would it not be judicious to draw near one who has an immensity of interest in us and who realizes how much we want to love her Son? Would

it not be wise to go to Mary who wants the friendship between Jesus and ourselves to be warm and fast
and lasting?

And so to Mary we must go if we want guidance
and suggestion. We read in the Book of Wisdom
words which could be applied to Mary: "Covet ye,
therefore, my words, and love them, and you shall
have instruction"; and again: "To think therefore
upon her, is perfect understanding, and he that watcheth for her, shall quickly be secure." Yes, we need
good counsel in our striving for constant friendship
with the Son of God—and Mary is the one whom we
should seek. To Nazareth we must make our journey.
There, with the noise and clamor of the world abated,
let us stay with Mary and listen closely to what she
has to say.

At Nazareth there will be little interruption. We
shall have time exclusively for Mary, something
which we do not have in our present state. Too many
voices drown out now the whisperings of Mary; too
many things claim attachment to our heart; so many
contingencies keep us from visiting her. The words
she speaks at Nazareth will truly help us, and her in-
dicative gestures, too. All of these will have much
meaning, but, most of all as time goes by, Mary will
stir the heart within us, sometimes without a word.
In gazing upon her, knowing that she brought God
to earth, seeing in her eyes a prevision of heaven, we

shall come to know that so far we have loved mistakenly, loved not the God we should hold dear, but loved, instead of Him, our meager selves. We shall sense the tenderness of Mary's natural affection for her Son, the rapture in her soul for Him who is her God. Perceiving this in Mary, we can well look back upon our past with wonder and dismay that we could have been so shortsighted and so wrong. Give up the struggle to become as little gods. Seek the "good counsel" of Mary, and return wholeheartedly to the living God.

Mother of Our Creator

THE BLESSED VIRGIN MARY has many brilliant gems in her diadem of glory and of honor, but possibly the one striking us most with awe is that signified by her title, "Mother of our Creator." Ordinarily we cannot fathom such a role for a human being. Our imagination fails, and only now and then in a breathless moment does our mind grasp this astounding reality. It comes in a spellbound instant when we are face to face with the fact that Mary, perfect woman made by God, is herself the mother of the same Creator.

It is far easier for us to see Mary in her relationship with her Son Jesus, both as a boy and as a man, for we have no difficulty in appreciating the natural bonds between mother and son. So, too, even with the Holy Spirit. We can understand quite normally how the Third Person of the Blessed Trinity would deal with her. We see this in the story of Annunciation Day. But being "mother of our Creator" produces, when the flashes of perception come, a solemn wonder and a reverential esteem at the fact of such grandeur and distinction. Yet, on the other hand, faith makes it sublimely simple to accept.

"Know that the Lord is God," writes the Psalmist, "he made us and we are his, his people and the sheep of his pasture." Think of Mary who through all her days had words like these burned upon her heart, who knew, of course, that she had been made from nothing, but whose whole being always was diffused throughout with the soul-stirring truth that she, and she of all the world, was the mother of the Creator. What rapture must uninterruptedly have filled her soul; yet what humility must have been hers when she was alone, "keeping all these things carefully in her heart"!

When we try to love God and be close to Him, we think usually of God in the Person of Jesus Christ. This is natural and is one of the reasons why the Son of God came down to earth, to draw us through Himself to the Father. But it would be wise for us in our devotions and our prayers to think more than we do of our Creator. God did create us. He made us out of nothing and placed us here on earth because of His unbounded love. This we know. But do we revert enough to the fact that at every instant He preserves our life, keeps our heart continually beating, and gives us the power to take every breath we breathe? God is our Creator, to be sure, but He is also our Preserver. And this is something to which we should give more thought, as we live out our expanse of days. "The Lord is in his holy temple," says the Psalmist, "his throne is in heaven. His eyes behold, his eyelids examine the children of men."

We wake up in the morning, alive and unscathed. It is God's ever watchful eye which preserves us from a multitude of catastrophes. Yes, God is our Creator and our Preserver, too. We should be more aware of His eternal interest in us and be more grateful to Him. A human mother does not merely produce a child and let it go at that, never more to heed the infant. Why, she spends a goodly portion of her life in sustaining her child. Similarly with our Creator and ourselves—only immeasurably more so.

If in our life of prayer we are forgetful of the Creator, because He is a spirit infinitely perfect, and find it difficult to appreciate Him and approach Him, then why not travel for a while and go to Nazareth where Mary lives? This is one of the most accessible ways to a further knowledge of God the Father to whom we attribute the work of creation. For at Nazareth we would see how days began in Mary's life and how days ended. In comparison we might have much food for reflection.

How could Mary awake to the dawn which her

Creator fashioned without immediately pondering upon the memory that she herself had helped to fashion the Creator, after the Child-God had been conceived in her womb? How could Mary witness the tenderness of night come down from the sky without recalling her own tenderness when the Body of Jesus came down from the cross? How could Mary go through the many hours of her day without raising her mind often to the God who had made her, without thanking Him with all her heart for letting Jesus abide with her?

On such little things we might meditate, and then contrast them with our own thoughts on the matter. How do we live our days and nights? Do we pause now and then to consider the majesty and bounty of God, our Creator? Listen to what the Psalmist says: "For who is God but the Lord? Or what rock is there but our God? God who has girt me with strength and made my way secure, who has made my feet swift as the feet of deer, and has set me upon high places, who has trained my hands for the battle, and my arms for bending the brazen bow. And thou hast given me thy saving shield, and thy right hand has sustained me, and thy care has made me great." Are these our thoughts as well?

At Nazareth we might revise our judgments; we estimate again the value of things we believe so necessary. We might find, as we conversed with Mary, "mother of our Creator," that we have hardly in the past even thanked God the Father for our gift of mortal life, without which we could not receive eternal life. A journey to Nazareth might be inconvenient, but recall that when Mary arrived there one day from Jerusalem, when her Son was twelve years old, she had God with her, never to lose Him again—until the cross of death. Is not this exactly what we want, too?

Mother of Our Savior

THE TITLE IN MARY'S LITANY with which we are
perhaps more affectionately acquainted, and the
significance of which we grasp with greatest ease, is
that of "mother of our Savior." The whole picture
seems to unfold, wherein we see again and again the
lives and love and tears of Mary and her precious
Son. We set our eyes once more upon all of Mary's
lifetime with Jesus, from the day an angel swept into
her room at Nazareth with words accredited by God,
until the day when she would hear her Son, our
Savior, deliver His final commission to the Apostles,
and then ascend to the right hand of the Father in
heaven. When we say "mother of our Savior," the
complete panorama passes before our view, and we
observe again the wondrous stillness of a night in
Bethlehem as well as the deathly stillness of an after-
noon in Calvary.

Far back in the daybreak of creation, Adam and

Eve, listening to the artful and mendacious ways of Satan, lost for themselves and all their heirs the marvelous gifts with which God had adorned them, gifts which in no way belonged to their nature, but were, instead, part of God's life only. They lost the grace of God, and we consequently are born without that state of sanctifying grace. We know that heaven cannot be secured without it. More than this, Adam and Eve had injured God, insulted Him, and only God could repair the injury done. So there came to earth the Son of God as Savior, and for His advent among men God chose Mary as His mother. "Of her was born Jesus," writes St. Matthew, "who is called Christ." Jesus means Savior; Christ means "the anointed one." St. Luke in the Acts of the Apostles, after describing the arrest of Peter and John, says that all their companions, with one accord, in a prayer to God the Father, refer to Jesus as "thy holy servant Jesus, whom thou hast anointed."

Here we are on earth knowing that someday we shall die. From our religious teaching we realize the purpose of this mortal life. It is a time of probation, a time during which we must prepare for heaven. Just as the angels were tested, so are we, except, instead of just one chance to prove their good will, we have many. The angels who sinned were never given another chance; we have opportunities for repentance time and time again. Yet, in looking at our past or even the present, what do we see there?

From the lower powers of our soul there comes occasionally, maybe often, the rising surging flow of one base passion or another. We know the rules of God laid down in His commandments. But despite this knowledge and despite the fact that either heaven or hell await us in eternity, we may let that passion shroud our mind and blind our will as we tread onward into sin. We walk away from God because down deeply we have not yet learned to receive our Savior totally in our heart. With our mind and will we know Him and confess Him, but the door to our heart has been barred, so that He has never been able completely to enter. This is why we sin. If Jesus possessed our heart, if He had a perfect freedom to move about within it, we could never lose the state of sanctifying grace. Yet Jesus, our Savior, knocks every night and day upon the entrance to our heart. He says in the words of Isaias the prophet: "Thou shalt know that I am the Lord thy Savior, and thy Redeemer."

Mary is the one, no doubt, whom we need. She understands our Savior intimately; she knows how intensely beats His Sacred Heart for our friendship. She notices how we keep closed to Him the portals of our heart. If we sincerely want always to live in our Savior's good graces, if we want to learn how

65

never to forsake Him, how to crush the passions of our lower nature when they rise to take command, then go to the Virgin Mother at Nazareth where we shall learn from her how thrilling, even in a human way, it can be to wage a campaign upon the battle-field of virtue, and how divinely consoling it can be to the soul.

In the Book of Deuteronomy we read: "When you go out to war against your enemies and you see horses and chariots and an army greater than your own, do not be afraid of them, for the Lord, your God, who brought you up from the land of Egypt, will be with you. When you are about to go into battle, the priest shall come forward and say to the soldiers: 'Hear, O Israel! Today you are going into battle against your enemies. Be not weakhearted or afraid; be neither alarmed nor frightened by them. For it is the Lord, your God, who goes with you to fight for you against your enemies and gives you victory.'"

Mary is the "mother of our Savior." She is await-ing us at Nazareth to remind us that we have a soul to save, and that her Son has come to help us. She will point out the reason why we fail Him, why we run away from Him. She will help us to open the gateway to our heart. As we listen to her, we per-haps shall realize how utterly strange it is that we, with all our supposed power and strength, should have to call on her, a gentle, graceful woman, to swing wide the door to that heart. How easily we have allowed others to enter therein, other loves, other affections, other adventurers! Mary will not condemn these other visitors. She will just explain that Christ comes first and, once He has possession, all else will follow and be welcome. After all, Mary is the "mother of our Savior"—not just mine alone.

Virgin Most Prudent

THE BLESSED VIRGIN MARY, immaculately conceived, was free always from the ravages and the remains of sin. She was the perfect creature, molded by the hand of God in a most special way. Her mind inherited from God on high the virtue of prudence which in her reflected so greatly His own providence; her will commanded thorough union with His own; her heart had love so unabated that she could with ease contain within her the secrets and the wonders of her God.

Mary was particularly thought of beforehand in Almighty God's mind, and when she was born of her mother, St. Anne, her soul was blessed with an excellence that flowered as she grew. The prudence that is of God had touched her soul.

Mary lived a great portion of her life with Jesus. Singularly blest with such closeness to God, she learned the ways of Jesus well, absorbed solid knowledge from Omniscience itself. And so Mary was all prudent. She had no need for the duplicity or diplomacy of man. And yet how much she could advise us if we went to Nazareth and stayed with her!

Much as we may think we know from our Catholic Faith about the mind of God, His will, His counsels and commandments, much as we are convinced of our understanding of our Savior Jesus and His redemptive life and death, we should scarce dare to think or say that no words from Mary's lips are needed to increase our belief. Despite our learning in the things of God, we are far away from Him at times in the folly of our thoughts, in our vacillating will and in our fickleness of heart. The virtue of prudence is one of the four great moral virtues implanted as a seed in our soul at the moment when we are baptized. In reality, it is upon prudence that all other virtues in a manner depend. How can we be charitable without it; or how can we be just to others? Charity does not consist in giving something to another, but in giving wisely, whether it be money or encouragement. Justice demands that we prudently respect another's rights as we exact our own due; it means, too, that we do not allow his exercise of right to be a transgression. This requires a discernment that has its source in God's mind, not in ours. Too, unless humility be guided by prudence, it can decline into obsequiousness, and fortitude can grow into the recklessness of a fool.

The virtue of prudence, developed properly within our soul, will keep us from excessive zeal which only embarrasses; it will raise us up from spiritual lethargy which destroys. Prudence makes us seek that which is good in God's eyes and far transcends the human prudence by which men on earth cleverly work out their aims. Prudence leads us also to a reverential fear of God which, of course, "is the beginning of wisdom." The Book of Proverbs offers this admonition: "If thou shalt call for wisdom, and incline thy heart to know prudence; if thou shalt seek her as money, and shalt dig for her as a treasure; then shalt thou understand the fear of the Lord, and shalt find the knowledge of God, because the Lord giveth wisdom: and out of his mouth cometh prudence and knowledge."

Life is not really the simple thing that it might be. We ourselves have made it complicated. Our motives, our plans and our ambitions have all entered into the scheme of life, and consequently our judgments and decisions are frequently not the wisest. We aim at a vague thing called happiness, and yet from experience we know that the pathway to it is not an artless one. We have to do some deft maneuvering and employ much human skill in order to reach the goal. The fact is, of course, that our conception of happiness may differ greatly from that of God's.

Too long, perhaps, have we been going our own way, and it is too bad that in our journeys we have not paused at Nazareth, the home of Mary. Inside that home dwells the "virgin most prudent," and what sound lessons we should learn there! Mary, who knows the mind of Christ so well, who knows what His desires are and what He wills, can so easily point out to us why real happiness may escape us. She can remind us again that real happiness is holiness, and that holiness is only the accepting and the doing of God's will always.

Try it some time. Go to Mary at Nazareth. Promise her renewed efforts to act graciously and without complaint, as Jesus wants us to act. It may be difficult at first, but gradually we shall learn that the prudence which is of God leads straight to happiness because it leads to holiness. With Mary we shall be neither unhappy, unholy nor unwise—ever. Why, then, not tarry at Nazareth awhile? Putting aside the deception that our own human prudence can be pitted against the providence of God, we shall simply step inside the house of Mary and listen to her say to us from the Book of Proverbs: "Whosoever is a little one, let him come in. Come, eat my bread, and drink the wine which I have mingled for you. Forsake childishness, and live, and walk by the ways of prudence."

There is much to be done in this life, and we are called upon by Jesus to do it. We are also warmly encouraged to do it by His mother. While prudence must govern our zeal so that we shall not be precipitate, at the same time we must never use prudence as an excuse for doing little or nothing. Prudence and an active working for God's purposes are not at all incompatible.

Virgin Most Venerable

THE BLESSED VIRGIN MOTHER has been revered by the Catholic Church from its very beginning, and her name has been enshrined in the hearts of the faithful even before the Church and the Apostles received their divine commission. Still ringing forth from the pages of the New Testament, in praise of the virgin mother, are the words of an unknown woman who had been listening to Jesus preach: "Blessed is the womb that bore thee, and the breasts that nursed thee." There is no need for Catholics to be told how essential Mary is in our lives. The Church has proclaimed her glories increasingly through the centuries, and we believe unquestioningly that Mary is in heaven, body and soul, and is the mediatrix of all graces that flow from the divine Heart of Jesus Christ.

Despite our faith in these prerogatives of Mary, however, and despite the fact that we should vigorously dispute any imputation against her, we do have to be reminded occasionally that we may lose for her some of that veneration and esteem which, as her children, we should always have. We may be guilty of forgetfulness of Mary, for example, by the hesitancy with which we have taken her admonitions at Fatima to heart. In many unknown and private ways we may be deeply devoted to Mary, but we can never really show too much respect for her. Perhaps we might increase our devotion by receiving Holy Communion on five consecutive Saturdays. Now, most Catholics recite the Rosary regularly, but how many of us can right now reach out and find our beads immediately at hand?

Mary holds a remarkable position in the Catholic Church, and the veneration which she receives, though stemming to a great extent from the tender love and affection which we have for her, is nevertheless based upon a sound and thorough study through the ages by the ablest of the Church's theologians. It is true that much of our regard for Mary results from the stirrings of our heart, and these feelings are all legitimate because basically they are rooted in the truth, arrived at by great minds within the Church and by the infallible declarations of St. Peter's successors.

"The Lord possessed me in the beginning of his ways, before he made anything from the beginning.

I was set up from eternity, and of old before the earth was made. I was with him forming all things; and was delighted every day, playing before him at all times; playing in the world." These words from the Book of Proverbs, written concerning the gift of wisdom, have been transferred by the Church to the lips of Mary. A more beautiful expression can hardly be found which portrays both the personal attraction toward Mary in our heart and, at the same time, the intellectual appreciation by our mind.

Mary has nobility of soul. She is the supreme example among creatures of goodness itself. This is one of the reasons why we call her "venerable." Mary shared in all the joys of Christ on earth—which is befitting—but she also experienced "the long dark night of the soul" when she was made to suffer bitter anguish. It is this blending of joy and grief in Mary's life, together with her modest consent to each as it came, that makes Mary the matchless woman she is. She was not afraid to scale the heights of heaven in knowing the delights of the Son of God, nor was she fearful either of draining the dregs offered to her by the Son of Man.

Yes, it is worth while to be reminded of Mary and her nobility of soul. Many lessons have we to learn from her, we who sometimes cannot take in stride the pleasures of life without excess, who cannot bear the pains of life without the whimper of a stricken prey.

If we reflect more upon Mary, we shall find at once that we are scarcely the reputable personages we are thought to be. This is why it would be good for us to go to Mary, whether we be sinner or saint. Nazareth in spirit is not far away. We shuffle back and forth on earth with indecision; we are often opportunists who feel complacent when we fulfill the minimum requirements of the moral law. We have good reason, then, to hasten on to Nazareth where we shall learn just what kind of person we are and what kind we can still hopefully become.

We can become a better person if we visit Mary's home and stay in spirit for some length of time. We shall be in the presence constantly of one who has nobility from God, who knew perfectly the moral law and equally accomplished it, who felt the uplifting power of God's eternal love amid the heartaches of her life on earth. We shall feel her subduing effect upon us. Quietly, silently and with dignity the beauty that is her soul will shine forth, and over us will come a tranquil and untroubled calmness, as we realize that we, too, can become more like Mary. We shall appreciate more deeply the moral stature she attained. We shall see more clearly our failures of the past and the reasons also why we have blundered. There will be at Nazareth a refinement of vision, a ventilation of the staleness of the past, and a spirit of hope which will add to our lives new zeal and new incentives for the affairs of God. All this can happen if we travel to Nazareth where lives our "virgin most venerable."

Virgin Most Renowned

THE FINEST AND THE ONLY true means by which mankind can attain heaven is adherence to the teachings of the Catholic Church. The Church is not an end in itself, but the means to an end. Because it is the pathway on earth whereby we may eventually find eternal bliss, there is expected of the Church certainty in the field both of morals and of truth. There can be no guesswork with the Church, no changing of Christ's teachings every now and then. In so important a work as a soul's salvation we have to be certain, and we believe that only the Catholic Church has remained completely faithful to the teachings of Christ. It is a great responsibility, this leading of mankind to God, and our Church is utterly cognizant of its grave moral obligation to all men. Hence the seeming rigor of the Church in its regard for the moral law, but a strictness no greater nor less

78

than that of Christ Himself; hence, too, its precise doctrinal teaching and its intolerance of error.

Emerging from all this supposed severity in its doctrinal and moral code is the beautiful tableau of the Virgin Mother and the renowned part she plays in the life of the Church. When Mary steps forward from this background of inflexibility, the cold language of dogma seems to gain a growing warmth, and hard rules concerning what we may do and may not do seem to soften into recipes of love. Not that Mary has caused changes in our doctrinal and moral beliefs, but, seeing her there among the Apostles and the Son of God himself, we tend to view things in another way, in Mary's way. Stringent regulations that seem at first to hem us in now become but words of love and yearning on the part of God for man. Listen to the Psalmist proclaim concerning God's laws: "Would that my way of life were set to observe thy laws! Then I shall not be counfounded, when I shall have respect for all thy commandments. I rejoice in the way of thy precepts, as much as in all riches. Open my eyes that I may give thought to the wonders of thy law. I am a stranger on the earth, hide not thy commandments from me. Protect me from the way of error, and grant thy law to me. O how I have loved thy law, O Lord! It is my meditation all the day."

In so critical an issue as our salvation, the truth of

Christ must be presented exactly as He taught it, and the moral law must not admit of deviations. For those who have gone astray through pleasure or through pride, the rules of God and Church appear to be impossibly hard, and many have "fallen by the wayside." Even those who love God much and prove it by good conduct may feel occasionally—at least regarding others rather than themselves—that the commandments may be just a little too uncompromising and final. All this musing betrays the fact that we are not yet perfect in this vale of tears, that we still think differently in some ways from God, and that as yet we are not always attuned to His holy will. Psychologically we may view the commandments of God and Church as decrees that limit freedom, whereas actually they are the sole guarantee of our liberty, both in time and in eternity.

It is not very easy always to see things this way. We constantly combat feelings that cry out for license and for looseness. We need some help in this respect. We need the aid of one who, being human, understands the ways of God. We need the aid of her who ran the gamut of emotion while she lived. We need the support of one who could have cried out against the most tragic crime of all, who bore within her soul, from starlit Bethlehem to starless Calvary, a nightmare of trial and the grim rack of a broken heart. We stand much in need of Mary who knows both the whims and phantasies of the human heart and the breathless impatience of Christ's Heart for the souls of men. We have to have Mary's great assistance in overcoming our tendency to view the moral law as a restriction instead of as an invitation to rest our head upon the breast of Christ and find disturbance nevermore.

The Virgin Mother is renowned above all creatures that have ever lived. She is renowned because of her own moral goodness, her position in the Church and, above all, because of her strikingly special prerogatives. She enjoyed all virtues and possessed them in a perfect measure. From heaven she has found herself and her status the object of prayerful inquiry on earth and research by the priestly minds of theologians through the ages. She is also renowned in the devotion afforded her by the Church whose beginnings she witnessed.

With all this in mind concerning Mary, we may hasten in spirit to her at Nazareth where she will be waiting, happy to see us. There we shall find ourselves with the most renowned woman in all of history. We shall be in quiet awe of her because of her wonderful privileges. She may be renowned specifically as mother of God and as a virgin immaculately conceived, but we shall recognize soon, as we look into her lovely face, that the main and general reason for her high renown is the reign she has over the human heart. Mary can make the most grievous sinner a saint; she can raise a generous soul to heights unknown.

So, we shall stay at Nazareth for a period of time. Mary can speak with us of God's commandments. How unhappy we have been when in the past we have secretly rebelled against these precepts! What have we gained? And how much we have lost in the way of grace! Listen closely to our "virgin most renowned," and feel our heart slowly surrender.

Virgin Most Powerful

Is it strange or unusual that the most powerful creature with God is a woman? Power is customarily associated with men, but that is physical, earthly power. To the ordinary fragility of Mary's womanhood God has added a strength to confound the mighty. Mary is the most glorious creature in the Church Triumphant today; nor should we be unmindful that on earth in the Church Militant she was a tremendous and inspiring force in the days of the early Church.

"Who shall find a valiant woman?", cries out Solomon in the Book of Proverbs, and the Catholic Church has indeed found her. "Strength and beauty are her clothing," Solomon continues, and Mary, we know, has beauty and power. In a world of men among whom religious wars have taken place and disputes still rage on, among whom power so often has swung the balance in swaying people to protest against the Catholic Faith, in a world that looks on physical force as the guarantee of anything and everything, and where dictatorships have shown such small concern for human carnage, the Catholic Church still holds Mary up before that world and shows her forth, despite it all, as a virgin and mother, the most powerful creature that has ever lived.

All power comes from God, and this we fully realize. We believe that all the saints of God have immense influence in interceding for us with God. But far and above all of those who have won their eternal reward stands the Blessed Virgin Mary to whom God has given such vast power that she alone, as co-redemptrix of mankind and under God, can obtain for each of us the graces Christ earned upon the cross of Calvary. Mediatrix of all graces, Mary in heaven can look back to her days on earth and live again in memory the joyful events of her life, and her glorious ones too; but it is because she stood on Calvary beneath Christ's cross and suffered tribulation of soul unequalled that today and everyday she can allot to our immortal souls the graces for which she asks, graces earned from Gethsemani to Calvary.

"The life of man upon earth is a warfare," says the Book of Job, and all of us know this. There are no saints without the scars of bitter battles on their souls. To know God as we should, to love and serve Him takes solid moral courage, and sadly we appreciate how weak and unresolved we are. No matter what our resolutions are, or how firm and purposeful, the struggle seems never to end, and our life becomes a repetition of moral failures large or small.

We are in battle on this earth for the salvation of our immortal soul. At all costs we must win heaven for eternity. At the end of life nothing else will matter in the least. The words of Jesus are so true: "What does it profit a man, if he gain the whole world, but suffer the loss of his own soul? Or what will a man give in exchange for his soul?" Naturally we should never hazard the chance of violating God's law now, in these our days, violations which can eventually deny us heaven. And yet, why is it that we do take chances? Well, first of all, we simply do not love God sufficiently, which in itself must always be regretted and a source of real concern. Secondly, the enemies we war against are not ones we can devastate by soldiery and armament. "Our wrestling," writes St. Paul, "is not against flesh and blood, but against the Principalities and the Powers, against the world-rulers of this darkness, against the spiritual forces of wickedness on high." The Principalities and the Powers are two of the ranks among angels, and those among them who fell with Lucifer were punished with hell. But they still roam the world with Satan of whom St. Peter writes: "Your adversary the devil, as a roaring lion, goes about seeking someone to devour."

Each and every one of us in this life seriously needs the grace of Christ, and, in securing this for us, Mary is the most powerful. In heaven our glorified Christ will heed most of all the imprecations and the requests of His mother on our behalf, but, what is even more, He gives these graces to her so that, wherever He wills, she with her own hands may allot them. Of ourselves, we are weaklings in the greatest crisis we shall ever face: the saving of our soul. We cannot afford to lose the battle, and, therefore, it becomes almost imperative that we go in spirit to Nazareth, and knock on the door of the home of Mary, asking her for the priceless help we need. She will open the door and welcome us inside. And there we may well be astounded at the strength of this blessed lady who, in her graciousness and womanliness, might appear to us fragile and soft. As we look at her, however, we shall be reminded of those crucial words uttered long ago by God Almighty to the serpent in Paradise: "I will put enmity between you and the woman, between your seed and her seed." At Nazareth we shall come to understand that Mary is locked in fierce combat with Lucifer until the end of time—and Jesus has assured His mother that she will be the victor.

We must be conquerors also. At Nazareth we shall live in Mary's house, but, more importantly, we shall begin to live Mary's life. The power which she has from God will immeasurably affect us. We shall see the secret of her power in the efficacy of sincere prayer. And if we shall learn from this "virgin most powerful" even only that lesson of prayer, then we shall have mastered the finest teaching of all. From then on, with Mary's help, we shall fight the battle of salvation on bended knees. For that is how it should be fought.

Virgin Most Merciful

THE CRY FROM EARTH perhaps most often heard within the courts of heaven is the plaint of human hearts for mercy. During our course of life we are beset with much affliction. We suffer from pain of body, or anguish of soul, or even from the pining of a lonesome heart. Most of us, no doubt, have called on Mary at these different times for help in easing the ache, or at least for courage in bearing it. No need is there to say here that we should pray to Mary, for our prayers are but the continuation of the pleas of those who have already lived their days on earth. As Mary has helped relieve the torment of our forebears by intercession with her Son, we, in turn, look to her as merciful beyond description.

The Virgin Mother must have for us a compassion about which we can only dream. She knows too well that we carry with us all through life a burden passed down from Adam. She knows, and with lament, that we have often failed our God, her Son, in breaking His commandments in order to follow our own pleasures and will. She knows that we have grievously done wrong in life, and have sometimes let long weeks go by, or maybe months, before we have sought forgiveness from her Christ. If, perhaps, we have added one sin to another over a long stretch of days and have long delayed our confession, Mary knows it. She is deeply aware of all this and must recall the words which her Son spoke in the Garden of Olives: "My soul is sad, even unto death." For although Mary has compassion on us, she also has compassion for Jesus and does not want Him hurt.

All of us have in the past asked Jesus to forgive us. With our religious training and the word of God expounded from pulpits during Mass, we are sufficiently aware that we have injured God when we sinned, and that we must do penance. Yet, Mary knows that many of us fail to realize how deeply we offend Jesus and how little of atonement we may actually make. Theoretically, we seem sound in the practice of our Faith, but down deep in our soul, where we should have compassion for the stricken Christ, there may be only systematic routine and the knowledge of principles. Since no soul ever felt for the wounded Christ on Calvary commiseration and sympathy which Mary felt, she wants to touch our heartstrings, to make us more familiar with the sufferings we have cost our God and the penance we must do in partial atonement.

Mary has sympathy for us who, because of a fallen nature, are sinful creatures; but Mary also has sympathy for the Heart of Jesus whom we offend by committing sin. Her aim would be to ease the feelings of the Sacred Heart, while gently touching our own hearts with the mercy of her Son, so that unison will exist between our Savior and ourselves in the doing of His will. Mary stands today near the throne of Christ in heaven, tenderly familiar with Him just as she was on earth, and even immeasurably more so. She does not want Him injured by our immoralities on earth, and she is ever ready to bring rapprochement between the desires of His Heart and the wavering loyalties of our own. She, above all creatures, conceived immaculate, knows how we are tempted to sin by the surging of our baser passions, and she has compassion for us, hoping that, among our cries for mercy, the one for the forgiveness of sin will be the most repeatedly heard. Mary understands our many weaknesses and, because of her merciful feelings toward us, she is so happy, even as Jesus is, when she hears from our lips the same prayer of the penitent sinner of whom the Psalmist speaks: "Have mercy on me, O Lord, for I am weak; heal me, O Lord, for my bones are troubled, and my soul is troubled exceedingly. Return, O Lord, rescue my soul, save me for thy mercy's sake."

We should perhaps think things over a little more than we do. We are conscious of our sinfulness as children of Adam, and much aware of our personal offenses against God. But are we too trite in our manifestations of sorrow before the living God? Do we act mechanically with regard to the sacraments? In receiving the Sacrament of Penance do we automatically depend upon Christ to accomplish His part in forgiving us, while we to an extent fail to acquire and to cultivate the dispositions demanded in receiving it? Is the penance imposed by the confessor too long, when a lifetime of penance would not be long enough?

Undoubtedly it would be beneficial for us if in spirit we visited Nazareth to spend some time with our "virgin most merciful." We should find that Mary's compassion for us far outweighs all the sympathy of earth, for she alone among all creatures understands the gravity of sin in its effect upon Jesus. And should we come to appreciate Mary's sympathy toward her Son, because she, alone of us all, knows how Christ is hurt by deliberate sin, we should begin to see things as she does.

If we were to spend such time with Mary, we should come back from Nazareth refreshed, with new thoughts in mind and more loving determinations of will. Perhaps our manner of seeking forgiveness would no longer be the automatic procedure, and, instead, we should come to realize that every time we stepped into the confessional, we were kneeling at Calvary before Christ on the cross. Mary would teach us that we are not the only ones who cry for mercy, that Jesus does also when He asks us not to sin. She would burn upon our memory the words of the Psalmist: "I have waited for someone to take pity, but there was no one, and for comforters, but I found none." That is the cry of Jesus. Why have we not heeded it before?

Virgin Most Faithful

IN THE WIDE SWEEPING PICTURE of our life which
has so far been a continuous attempt to keep God's
holy will, we find scattered here and there occasional
moral failures. Even yet, in trying to lead a life of
virtue, we find ourselves disposed and prone toward
deeds that should not be. As we look back upon our
personal sins, we can in certain instances discover the
specific reason why we did the wrong, but, in general,
the ground upon which the edifice of evil in our life
has been constructed is that of non-observance of the
covenant or pact which God has made with each of us
as individuals. God has made wonderful promises to
us, and we at baptism through our sponsors once
pledged our word to God. Through them we re-
nounced Satan, his works and all his pomps. Incidentally, this is why the Church insists on godparents
who are good and practicing Catholics, for only they
by good example can help lead a child to God. But

that we have disowned the devil and his display is a fact.

What has happened to us since? Why the sloth in our lives, or the anger? Why the avarice, why the pride? Is it not truly because we have forgotten our contract with God? The Almighty still keeps His part of the bargain. The Son of God is here sacramentally on earth, ever to be with us. He has promised heaven if we but love Him and keep His laws. If unfortunately we fail in moral decisions, Christ is in the confessional to forgive us. When the daylight of the sky grows faint and we are passing our last hours on earth, He leans over us through His priests and anoints us with holy oil, soothing our path to His throne of judgment. Yet, we have so often evaded the terms of our contract. We chose Satan again, and his machinations. In other words, we have been unfaithful; we have broken our promises; we have been disloyal. Perhaps we need to learn the lesson of faithfulness over again, at least as far as it pertains to God. "Son," says the Book of Ecclesiasticus, "when thou comest to the service of God, stand in justice and in fear, and prepare thy soul for temptation. Take all that shall be brought upon thee; and in thy sorrow endure, and in thy humiliation keep patience. Keep his fear, and grow old therein."

We honor human contracts to the best of our ability in business and finance, in social life and in marriage. But somewhere along the way we may have lost a sense of responsibility in respecting the contract we have made with our Maker. The Church itself enabled us to enter into this covenant with God in our earliest days, when it took us at baptism from the state of original sin and placed us in that of sanctifying grace. This state of grace, wherein God makes it possible for us to share in His life and even pledges His kind of happiness for eternity, demands on our own part a faithfulness to His wishes and commandments. In general we break down in the matter of fidelity. We have simply forgotten the terms of the contract we made with God on our baptismal day.

It may be necessary that we take another look at our situation, that we revise our thinking, and that we point our finger at the main occasion of our sins. We, who are so faithful to men and at times so unfaithful to God, should in spirit travel to the home of Mary in Nazareth where we can meet our "virgin most faithful." By virtue of her special dignity she, of all human creation, was most faithful to God and is the most faithful to man. It would be heartening to remain with the virgin mother for a time, and learn that the battle for salvation, though possibly a complicated and perilous one, can be rather simple, if we understand some fundamental truths.

Let Mary remind us that she was not the only one blessed with the presence of Jesus in her home; physically, yes, but we also can have Him every day in Holy Communion. Mary would have us keep in mind that she herself never left Jesus when life became difficult. She could well remind us that we ourselves do leave Him, and she could ask us, too, if we have noticed, when things seem to go wrong and we become discouraged, that Satan comes with all his pretense and parade to offer us the consolation he once held out to Eve: "God knows that when you eat of the fruit of the forbidden tree, your eyes will be opened and you will be like God." She will tell us, if we wish to remain welcome in her home, that we shall have to honor our baptismal vows. She will caution us against being deceived by Satan and will offer us her tremendous help. Mary is the foremost and most formidable opponent whom Lucifer has, and she can place her weapons in our hands if we finally decide to listen to the Evil One no longer.

It is entirely this simple: a question of faithfulness; a problem of our word. Of course, we shall ever be tempted, and we shall yield easily to temptation whenever we lose sight of that contract we once made with God. We cannot remain faithful by ourselves alone. We need the grace of Christ, and Mary is certain to obtain that help at the throne of her Son in heaven. But she has to hear first our set and sealed decision.

What shall we gain by our unwillingness to live up

to terms? A few paltry pleasures at the most? But what shall we lose? The haven of Mary's faithful heart, and her home as well. We lose our Savior Jesus, too, if we leave Mary, unresolved. Think it over again. Where is our honor?

Mirror of Justice

OF ALL HUMAN CREATURES Mary suffered most
from the injustices of men. With their unhal-
lowed minds and perverted wills, men robbed Mary
of her Son, her God. They persecuted Him, lied
about Him, set traps for Him, condemned Him at a
farcical trial, tortured Him and put Him to death.
Mary was not simply a bystander at all of this, nor
was she simply an acquaintance, nor simply a close
friend. She was His mother who had trudged all the
way from Nazareth to Bethlehem in order to bring
Jesus into this world of unjust men. She was His
mother, and she felt the rebuff of Bethlehem and the
backlash of Calvary. In the intervening years she
brooked the blasphemy of Pharisees and the hypoc-
risy of Scribes. She, who of all the world was the
least deserving of asperity and brutishness, was called
upon by God to bear the brunt of man's injustice
toward God's Son and her own. Mary shared ex-

quisitely in every happiness of Jesus, but, as His mother, she suffered so much with Him through His trials and through His passion. How much the ordinary woman will suffer in sympathy with an afflicted son, but how limitlessly more so must has been the grief of Mary whose own Son is God's own Son and whose agony brought her martyrdom itself! Among the Lamentations of Jeremias in the Old Testament we read these soft but poignant words, often applied to the Virgin Mary: "O all ye that pass by the way, attend, and see if there be any sorrow like to my sorrow."

If we explore the undercurrent of this travail which Jesus and Mary bore, we find as its cause not the isolated incidents of which the Gospels speak, nor even the evil deeds perpetrated on Christ's Person, but we find rather the awful injustice that lies within the heart of man. What a wonderful world this would be if each of us sought to give to another what is due him! Instead, as we know too well, there dwells within the lower regions of our soul a fierce craving for our own pretensions and prescriptions.

Let us not pretend on an issue such as this. It is our own rights we want maintained; hardly ever at our own expense the rights of others. We are insistent on receiving sometimes what is more than our due, but reluctant that our neighbor acquire even that which belongs to him if we are in any way to be deprived. Too often we think exclusively of ourselves and let others fall where they may. In business we can climb over them by our guile; in competition, perhaps, by our cheating. Even in the intimate area of marriage, where two become one, how often we think of ourselves alone as *the* one. What damage is wrought by the spouse who has little concern for the rights of a partner. Harken to the words of the Book of Ecclesiasticus: "Let not thy hand be stretched out to receive, and shut when thou shouldst give." If only we could learn early enough that life's genuine joy is found in giving, not in getting!

What evils, too, have been caused by human tongues! How quickly a reputation can die or a good name be lost by the jaundiced eye of another! How bitterly narrow the heart which will permit the ruin, with a few deft stabs, of the hard-earned reward of a brother! How many crushed souls there are which are made desolate by the criminal sermonizing of the babbler who frequently would do, if he could, the very things of which he accuses the other! "Deceit," says the Psalmist, "is in the heart of them that think evil things. Lying lips are an abomination to the Lord. For the sins of the lips, ruin draweth near to the evil man."

Perhaps we should visit in spirit the home of Mary in Nazareth. We who may have felt the sting of the reviler, who have been unjustly accused or hurt by a pietist's preachment, will find words with Mary most revealing. Let her tell us the story of her early days, which Matthew relates in his Gospel, the story of how "she who had been betrothed to Joseph, before they came together, was found to be with child by the Holy Spirit. But Joseph her husband, being a just man, and not wishing to expose her to reproach, was minded to put her away privately." This was embarrassing for Mary, and especially because of her high degree of holiness.

Mary will tell us how she bore this temporary shame: she simply offered up her trial to God. And then what happened? An angel took care of it all. Mary will ask us to bear injustice resignedly and without murmur. In due time she herself will take the angel's part. We shall feel stronger and calmer in bearing injustice without complaint.

Seat of Wisdom

THE TITLE, "seat of wisdom," with which the Church addresses Mary in her litany, is probably the most majestic one of all. It adds the fullest stature to her dignity and contributes most perhaps to her nobility of soul. To have the wisdom of God is to be blest immensely, but to be the very "seat of wisdom" is to dwell in heaven nearest to the throne of Jesus, nearer than all the angels, closer than the holiest of saints. It is to share as perfectly as a human creature can in that great gift of the Holy Spirit which the Church calls "wisdom." It is wisdom, too, which makes man so relish the things of God that he loses all taste for things of this world, except as they are necessary for his service to God.

Of course, while Mary lived at Nazareth, she was never at a great distance physically from Jesus. She had first heard the beat of His tiny Heart in the sanctuary of her own womb, and how often she could tell that beat as she fled into far off Egypt, holding her Infant Child in her arms! All through His days and nights with her, Christ's Heart was near, until the day on Calvary when a soldier's lance went through His frame and pierced the Heart she had so adored.

Not only was Mary physically within reach of His Heart, but spiritually, too, in a much more intimate way. "With me," says the Book of Proverbs, "are riches and glory, glorious riches and justice. For my fruit is better than gold and the precious stone, and my blossoms than choice silver." Nazareth for Mary was rather a prelude to heaven, except for the tears she may have shed. She must have thanked Him openly and often for His munificence to her; and then think of the many favors she must have asked of Him on behalf of her friends. Mary saw at its finest the wisdom of Christ on earth and was herself seized by it to an astonishing degree. Her whole life became a ceaseless desire for Him, for the things of God and for souls. And today in glory Mary is the very "seat of wisdom," officially termed so by the Church.

How greatly in need are we of this taste for things divine! Avid for the heirlooms of time, for ownership, for comfort and for pleasure, we want security as our major aim. But notice where we look for it. We act as if our security depended just on ourselves, and really it does if we are not content with what God gives us. Would that we were wise with the wisdom of God! Then we should not strain in frenzy to gain the things which we believe are needed for happiness; then we should be satisfied with only the tangible which God knows can bring us joy. But we fail to see eye to eye with God. We forget that real wisdom is a relish for God's interests, and we wear ourselves out in trying to obtain our own. The Book of Proverbs says, "O children, how long will you love childishness, and fools covet those things which are hurtful to themselves, and the unwise hate knowledge?"

All of us, without question, wish hopefully that we were morally better than we are. No one wants to be bad. But to strengthen our link with Jesus and to approach Him more closely takes work and effort on our part. Who among us does not wish to understand Christ better, but how few take the means to learn more about Him? To love Jesus demands a concern more with Him than for self, demands a preference more for our oblation to Him rather than for His favors to us. But how many have the courage to move this way? Almost every one wants to serve Christ more faithfully, but, at the moment of decision, how important do those things suddenly become which bring us prominence, or contentment to our will, or perhaps forbidden pleasures to our flesh? Yes, most of us want to be better and to love Christ more; but the cost is high, and we frequently delude ourselves into believing that we cannot afford the price.

How greatly we need to go in spirit to Mary and stay with her for awhile. We are so frivolous, we children of Adam, and have need for the wisdom of the Holy Spirit. Mary is the "seat of wisdom," through whose hand flows all the sharing in this gift. We shall not learn from her in a day. It all takes time, but the longer in spirit we remain with her, the more ardor we shall have for the things of God. At Nazareth she will repeat to us words from the Book of Proverbs, words concerning wisdom, but which have been applied by the Church to herself: "Blessed is the man that heareth me, and that watcheth daily at my gates, and waiteth at the posts of my doors. He that shall find me, shall find life, and shall have salvation from the Lord. Whosoever is a little one, let him come to me."

In our worldly wisdom we have made mistakes; in our discretions we have erred. But we are still inclined to depend upon ourselves and our own calculations in our search for happiness and security. If we continue to rely upon ourselves alone, we shall blunder again. Why not then reach out to Mary and begin to know the wisdom of our God inside our hearts? How futilely we have struggled in the past for our objectives! Why not let God bring us happiness and security in His way? Let Mary, as the "seat of wisdom," remind us of our startling lack of confidence in God. By listening to Mary's counsel and praying with her, we shall know a joy that we may not have tasted yet. We shall even smile with Mary and have laughter. When we reach that stage, then we shall be truly wise.

Cause of Our Joy

OUR CATHOLIC PEOPLE and priests need not be reminded of the joy which the Blessed Virgin
Mary has brought to devout souls in the Church. In
reading the lives of the saints we are struck with the
fact that always, despite the bitter hardships so com-
monly found in their lives, they have been in heart
the most joyful of all men and women. No one has
become a saint without prostration of soul, and no
saint failed to enjoy inner peace in his darkest day.
In the eyes of saints, no matter what took place, God's
will was being done. He was running the show of
life; they were not, and their spiritual exaltation rested
on that premise alone.

There is a remarkable difference between the joy
of the world and that peace of which Christ says,
"Peace I leave with you, my peace I give to you; not
as the world gives do I give to you." Human joy is
passing, never constant, dies too quickly. All we can

ever retain is its memory. Spiritual joy is of the soul, need never pass away, and knows not melancholy even in life's darkest hour. The Psalmist says to God so beautifully: "Thou hast put more joy in my heart than that of those who are rich in grain and wine. As soon as I lie down, I fall asleep in peace, since thou alone, O Lord, hast settled me in security."

Is not this what we want most of all, the joy of peace and security? Is not our entire life directed toward its attainment? And yet where have we been seeking this joy? Often perhaps we have wandered into the bypaths of the world in search of diversion, excitement and flame. There is a passing joy to it all, passing like the moon at dawn. There still remains the fever inside us, the restlessness, the tempest which the world and its spirit can never satisfy. And all the time real joy lies latently in our heart, and we have not sought it there. Because of his search for happiness man moves to other climates, other regions; he changes jobs and even wives; he seeks it in a colorful theater stage or in dissembling books. He looks for it in flattery and unctious words. But never does he seem to realize that all the time his greatest possibility of joy lies in himself.

This condition is true with so many of us. We look for joy in fields afar, in any field but our own. We think that change and new positions, even new faces, can bring us the peace we seek. We seem to

act as if happiness depended fully upon outer elements. Yet we shall find out some day that genuine
joy can be found most of all within ourselves, pro-
vided, of course, that Jesus Christ is in our heart. He
must be there, just as we, with the beloved Apostle
John, must also be able to lean our head upon His
shoulder. We have seen people like this in the course
of life. They may have little of life's good fortune,
or not. To them such consideration makes little difference. They are satisfied with what they possess
and with what they are. They have accepted willingly God's decision in their regard and, as a result,
they are people of charm and gentility, of graciousness and culture, of disarming simplicity. Their
awareness of where real joy is found has made them
this way. When we meet them we are somewhat
taken aback, for their contentment points a caution-
ing finger at us, our ambition and coveting. The
Book of Ecclesiasticus reminds us that "The life of a
laborer that is content with what he hath shall be
sweet, and in it thou shalt find a treasure."

The Virgin Mary can be the real "cause of our
joy," if we but let her. While we still have the time,
why not in spirit see her at Nazareth, where we shall
learn what substantial joy really is, and how artificial
are the enjoyments which we have been tasting.
Mary has Jesus, and has possessed Him always. She
never of herself let Him go. This is why Mary, while

on earth, was the most joyful of God's creatures, why today in heaven she is the "cause of our joy." Mary will help us to retrace the pattern of our lives, recalling to us that whenever we sought delights apart from Jesus, we were doomed to disappointment. She will remind us again of the truth which we may have forgotten, that, although we may have wandered, His voice is always with us—the voice of conscience. Through sin we may lose Jesus, but not the sound of His voice. And this is why we are not happy when we think we should be.

Mary knows that down deep we want to be morally good and faithful to Jesus, but she also knows that when promptings arise within us to relieve the drab monotony of living, we immediately tend to look about on the outside for that deliverance. Mary will tell us that we fall into sin simply because we have never really risen from it. Our tie to Jesus, she will say, is perhaps strictly a conversational one, more that of an acquaintance than that of a friend. She will repeat for our benefit the words of Isaias the prophet: "This people honors me with their lips, but their heart is far from me."

Mary will urge us to stay in spirit with her for a time, to see the joy permeating her home and the hearts of the Holy Family, and later she will ask us to compare our little joys with hers. The Church says

110

that she is the "cause of our joy," and yet for so long have we been returning to spurious causes. We shall realize from her that true joy cannot be found without Jesus, nor the pleasure of sin with Him.

Spiritual Vessel

M AN IS A COMBINATION of the spiritual and the physical. He has an immortal soul and a perishable body. True, he is not like the angels who are spirit only, God's first rational creatures; but he does stand high in God's estimation. Listen to what the Psalmist says about man: "What is man, that thou art mindful of him or the son of man, that thou art concerned about him? And thou hast made him a little less than the angels, thou hast crowned him with glory and honor; thou hast given him power over the works of thy hands, thou hast placed all things under his feet."

We have to live in this world of material things because God wills it that way. He gave us a body which has to be cared for as well as a soul which has to be saved. The material elements in this world are therefore good, for they were made by God and placed here for our use. We go wrong when we fail to use them properly, when we neglect to use them for God's honor and glory. With surplus wealth, are we charitable or do we hoard it for ourselves alone? With marital pleasure, do we help God create or do we seek pleasure for its own sake? So, too, with food and drink, and with all creatures of God—how do we use them?

Our soul, we know, is the important fabric of God's personal creation. It is, after all, our very self. It is because of our soul that we think and choose and remember, that we weep and laugh, and love and hate. It is with our soul that we strive upward toward the everlasting God or select instead to satisfy the persuasive call of lower cravings. Either our soul rules our body, and we can serve God well, or, instead, our flesh can wear the crown, and then we are but slaves. We are always anxious with regard to our physical health and careful that our food be of the best; but how little vigilant are we at times concerning that with which we nourish our soul. We who would not dare have our children drink any milk but the best, are we as watchful over what their souls drink in, as interested in preventing poisoning of their souls as of their bodies?

When we think of it, we fail often in things of the spirit, at least in comparison to things of the flesh. God made us, first of all, to know Him; yet how few of us are attempting to understand Him as we ought.

We have ever near us the Christ of whom even an eternity of constantly increasing revelation in heaven will not be enough, and how seldom do we turn on earth the pages of a spiritual book to find out more about Him? If we take a close look at ourselves, many of us may find that we are not troubling to know Christ at all. These are not simply words; they are the truth.

The spiritual aim of our life must be high. We cannot afford to lower our sights, particularly when our objective is heaven. We must not make the mistake of thinking that the state of grace is attained in its fullest just by our keeping free from mortal sin. The spiritual life requires much more than that. It demands a positive effort on our part to love God and to strengthen that love as time goes by. Consider our prayer life. Have we stopped praying every day? St. Paul told the Thessalonians: "Pray without ceasing." Have we ignored his advice? Or have we forgotten the night outside the Garden of Gethsemani when Our Lord said to His Apostles, "Sit down here, while I pray"? If Christ Himself would pray to His Father in heaven, not only on this occasion but so very often, how self-sufficient have we become that we need no prayer at all? Are we feeding our soul with good food at Mass, or do we simply remain there without uttering a prayer? Are we among those who think the sacraments of the Church are for others, not for ourselves? Perhaps, after all, we need Mary, and need her much, for no one could point out better than she how stagnant the life of our soul may have become.

A visit to Mary at Nazareth would be to see the virgin who made her entire life a continuous prayer. How could she be other than the most prayerful being who has ever lived, she who is mother of God? And the Church calls her "spiritual vessel." Mary would see our soul as we approached her, blighted perhaps, producing no harvest, untilled and not much cared for, greatly in need of sunshine and fresh air. She might describe our condition by quoting these words of the Psalmist: "My soul lies prostrate in the dust: restore life to me according to thy word."

Mary would refresh us with the truth that our soul has been made like to God, and would encourage us to do everything possible in effecting a more affectionate union with Him. She will offer us her Son Jesus as a brother and a companion and tell us how, if we but knew Him better, we would no longer wish to follow the illicit promptings of our lower nature, would even come to desire a deeper spiritual life and look upon the state of grace as our most precious treasure, even anticipating our advance along the pathway of the saints. Mary would show us their footprints on the adventurous road of virtue, love and dedication. With her by our side, we should almost

115

welcome all that this pathway entails—the discipline, the hardship and the cross of Christ itself. There is no way to real happiness on earth or eternal joy in heaven without the spirit of the cross in our lives. And with Mary we should finally find it.

Vessel of Honor

IN THIS LIFE WE SEE so often the morally good being chastened, and the bad apparently coming off
rather well. They who are morally bad—the unscru-
pulous person, the liar, the hypocrite, the wolf in
sheep's clothing—all seem to have a sufficiency of
this world's goods. And it seems that "they who
hear the word of God, and welcome it" often suffer
privation, humiliation or even the impairment of good
name. The difference, of course, lies in honor. The
good can be happy in their adversity; the bad in their
heart can be wretched. The Book of Proverbs says,
"Whatever shall befall the just man, it shall not make
him sad; but the wicked shall be filled with mischief."

There are some things more valuable to us than all
the possessions we may hold in our hand. They are
the ones we hold in our heart. Integrity, a good
name, courage, dignity and purity of heart are moral
qualities which enable a man to hold high his head,

to look the world straight in the eye, and to carry within him a heart that is free from the burden of guile. Virtue has its own sublime recompense, for it makes men and women forget what they have, rejoicing more over what they are. They are honorable, and not only do others secretly respect them, but they respect themselves, which is of much more consequence. They who continually try to lead a life of virtue, despite temptation and material loss, can with joyous hope listen to these words of David, the king, in his fourteenth psalm: "O Lord, who shall dwell in thy tabernacle, who shall live on thy holy mountain? He who walks without sin and works justice and thinks uprightly in his heart, and does not slander with his tongue; who does no evil to his neighbor nor casts reproach upon his comrade; who holds the sinner in contempt and honors those who fear the Lord; who, although he has taken an oath with loss to himself, does not retract it, nor does he put his money out to usury, nor take bribes against the innocent. He who does these things shall not be moved forever." What a consolation to know that, as we grow older in the ceaseless moving of time, God is looking down from His heaven, reading our hearts, perceiving what we wish and hope for above everything else, seeing us attempt the good so valiantly when we are ever surrounded by the bad!

Above all human creatures stands the holy virgin

Mary whom the Church calls "vessel of honor." Mary represents every virtue which we should like to acquire, every good quality which we wish to have. On earth Mary had a perfect sense of what is true and right and just. She lived with God Himself and saw in Him, to a degree more clearly than any one else could, "the way, and the truth, and the life." There is a wonderful manifestation of respect in calling her "vessel of honor," for it portrays to us Mary's sterling worth both to the Church itself and to the faithful of that Church who so intimately know her. Mary's good name is enthroned both in the archways of the sky and in the hearts of men, for she herself holds a position unequaled by any other human either in heaven or on earth.

Mary is God's mother, a marvelous reality we all know, but a truth that startles our imagination. No matter how much we conjure up the vision of a woman giving birth to God, our inspiration fails. It is only when we think of Jesus, walking this earth, living and breathing like any created soul, that our mind comes back to earth from cloudland, and we know with utter certainty that Mary is God's mother. Her virginity also, perpetual and undeniable, shines forth amid all the glories of heaven, as it does even today in the shrine of human hearts on earth. Because of these great privileges Mary ranks in highest esteem,

119

and the reflection of this admiration is found in our own veneration for her, in our fealty and regard.

Most of us, of course, could abide a briefing with regard to honor. Living in the manner of the world and being a part of it as we are, we may have lost sight in our own lives of that which is just, true and right. Perhaps we have done no serious wrong, but we may have lowered our standards somewhat concerning our relationships with God and with man. The high idealism which once we possessed may have lessened along the way, and it is possible that we live now according to valuations far below that of former days, perhaps according to the canons of convention rather than of the moral law. This is why it would seem strange that we should hesitate to go to Mary, who is God's precious vessel of the honor which we ourselves may have lost.

So, why not in spirit depart for Mary's home in Nazareth, with the hope and assurance that we can regain the integrity and the candor which we may have squandered. It is never too late to become again the person we once were in younger times, when blood ran fresh and our heart was of oak. In her own sedate and demure way Mary will teach us that honor comes before all else, honor with God and also among men. She will tell us that there is no greater feeling of joy or intellectual conviction of humble supremacy than the gift of honor, which is really no gift at all. It is

120

rather an acquired and practiced simplicity of life and singleness of aim which is in absolute conformity with what God wants.

At Nazareth we shall remain, and the ideals we may have almost forgotten will be recovered. We shall look at Mary as we once did in our early childhood days, and we shall wonder how we could have ever gone so far away from her. But we shall not worry. Mary will unseal her "vessel of honor," and we shall never be the same again.

Singular Vessel of Devotion

THE ONE PERSON whose devotion to the Son of God on earth exceeded that of any other was certainly the Blessed Virgin Mother. Naturally she cherished and loved her Child Jesus in a human way when He was but an infant, and the memories of the months, particularly from Annunciation Day to Bethlehem, must have been indelible ones indeed, memories vivid through all the rest of her life. Every mother innately has great affection and love for the child of her womb, and Mary enjoyed this same natural emotion, but on a much greater scale, for she could hardly erase from her mind the fact that this little Child, with whom she played and smiled and whom she taught to pray, was the majestic God Himself. And so her maternal feelings were a mixture of the natural contentedness of any woman who bears a child in love and the unearthly triumph of being the one woman who had borne her God in love.

Beyond and above these normal emotions that flowed through the heart of Mary, there was her remarkable devotion of soul to Jesus, Son of God, who was walking the earth now among men. His haven of respite from the campaign of the day was her own humble abode in Nazareth to which He so often repaired. Mary was His choice and "singular vessel of devotion." She was our Lord's first congregation, praising Him silently with hymns in her heart and offering Him the oblation of her very self. From the first moment when the Son of God entered her womb, before the centurion would in later years cry out at the cross, "Truly he was the Son of God," Mary acknowledged His divinity and, with all the totality of a mother's libation, poured out her soul to be consumed by His.

Now it is true that we may look upon ourselves as a people much devoted to the service of God, but it is also a fact that most of us limit that service to Mass on Sunday. We are, of course, a busy people, and no great amount of time remains after the duties and work of a day. However, somewhere along the way, is it possible that we have lost that sense of personal devotion which is so characteristic of one who loves Jesus? In a way we can detect our earnestness by our attitude at Mass which should be the center of all of our devotional life. Do we pray the Mass? Do we think seriously while it lasts that Christ Himself, through the ministry of a priest, is offering again His own body and blood to His Father in heaven? And that we should be joining therein by offering our mind and our will? "Receive," says the priest in part when he offers the bread on the paten, "Almighty and Everlasting God, this spotless host, which I, Thy unworthy servant offer unto Thee, my living and true God, for my countless sins, trespasses and omissions." There is more to this prayer, but these words are enough for just now to make us wonder if we recall at that moment, and with any real sorrow, the many times we have hurt God in the past. Are we lifting our mind and our heart toward God as the words of consecration go hurriedly by? Or are we barren of thought, empty of words, and unable to feel even sympathy with the Christ who sacramentally still takes the burden of our infidelities upon Himself?

Most of us wish that our spiritual life had more unction and fervor, but so many of us are careless about giving some time to acquire this habit of reverent reflection. It is difficult for our mind to create heavenly thinking without first, then continually, nurturing our mind with holy food acquired from devout reading. Even one minute a day with a book of devotion would help us gradually to free ourselves from the morass of earth, would enable us in time to dwell with ease and simplicity upon eternal things.

And how changed for the better would our life become little by little! Our thoughts would harbor unfading truths; our lips would reveal spiritual soundness and health; and our deeds would turn to our credit and carry us into heaven. We read in the Book of Proverbs: "He that tilleth his ground shall be filled with bread; but he that followeth idleness shall be filled with poverty." What about us and the field of our soul which we may not be tilling?

Mary, we know, is our "singular vessel of devotion." She is unique in her appreciation of Jesus and in her exchange of intimate conversation with Him. We might in spirit move over to Nazareth and stay with Our Blessed Lady for a period of time. We who need so much the counseling whisper of Jesus must first learn to talk with Him as an intimate friend. Sometimes we find ourselves almost estranged from Him, and we certainly do not desire such an impasse to remain. Speak to Mary about it. Ask her where we fail, and why. She will tell us to look deep within our heart where stand our loves and our affections. Mary will caution us that it is easy to accept Jesus with our intellect, but that our heart may be crowded with too much fondness and fancy for others to permit Him admittance. This could be why our heart is cold toward Him, why our prayer to Him lacks any endearment. She will tell us that we are much in error if we think human love is more satisfying than the divine, and she will quote for us the words of the Psalmist: "One day in thy courts is better than a thousand others. I would rather stand upon the threshold of the house of my God, than dwell in the tents of sinners."

Then there will come the day, if we spend time with Mary, when we, too, shall echo the Psalmist with these words: "How lovely is thy dwelling, O Lord of Hosts! My soul longs for, fainting, it eagerly covets the courts of the Lord." And Mary can see to it that we walk the corridors of God forever.

Mystical Rose

WE ARE ALL FAMILIAR with the manifold significance of a rose. Though other flowers may
be more dazzling, exotic or colorful, still the rose in
our culture is considered as the most elegant of all.
Its solid complexion gives it richness, and its conserva-
tive but vibrant hue bring it a worth more authenti-
cally lasting. All flowers bring brightness and cheer,
but the rose brings a luster and joy which is almost
illusive and implied. Most flowers in the hand of a
giver signify affection or sympathy, whereas the rose
signifies a love and a warmth that may lie rather deep.
Other flowers seem to bespeak on the part of the do-
nor a simple cheerful wish of greeting, a hello with
a goodbye; but a rose seems to convey from the giver
a desire to leave his heart behind and not really to
say farewell. It is like the candle offered in a church
by one who must be on his way, but who wants the

Lord to know that his thoughts and feelings are still there.

Our Blessed Lady is likened to the rose and is symbolically called "mystical rose" by her Church. Of course, there is exclusively a spiritual import here, which is neither apparent to the senses nor obvious to the mind. But there is reality here, for Mary has the position among human creatures similar, in a way, to that which the rose has among all flowers. Other friends of God may have led more humanly dramatic lives, may have done deeds of daring for the cause of religion which would win medals today, may have physically suffered for Christ in a more intense measure, may even have offered their heads on the block. But Mary, unknown for her exploits, continually and constantly from her early days was the person of mettle above all others, the one with the staunchest heart of grace, the one undiscernibly living a more vividly dramatic existence, and the one more a martyr in soul than all of the blessed souls who followed to the end these words of Jesus: "He who would save his life will lose it; but he who loses his life will find it."

Mary, in her universal appeal to the entire Church of Christ, has the same deep flush as the rose. True, she has the delicacy of other flowers, their freshness and their array, but above all these, in her unmistakable value to the hearts of men and women and in her concern for them, she wears so softly, yet so strikingly, the countenance of the rose. She has a permanency about her, a sense of indispensability to the Church and to us as members of the Church. Mary is only a creature just as we all are, but the providential hand of God has raised her to a pinnacle upon this earth, and she stands supremely alone. Yet, from that vantage ground midway between God and ourselves, Mary fulfills her great destiny, by persuasively directing our attention and affections toward her Son, and by taking up our cause before His throne in heaven. In words written about the gift of wisdom, but which the Church puts on the lips of Mary, the Book of Ecclesiasticus says, "I was exalted . . . as a rose plant in Jericho."

Fundamentally all of us wish that we could love Christ more and serve Him in a more perfect way. As sinners, we are discontented with ourselves or, if we are reasonably trying to link our minds and hearts with Christ, it is inevitable that we are never satisfied with the limitations of our desires and efforts. But in either case, whether seriously for the first time we are beginning to tread the path toward Christ or are by now well acquainted with that road through years of effort, we need in the garden of our devotional life not only the spontaneity and vivacity and variety suggested by many flowers, but the endurance and tender perseverance expressed by the rose. We need again to remember as well that our friendship

129

with Jesus, though helped by public worship and the Church's liturgy, is more nurtured and fostered and sustained by our own sincere private prayer and by our personal affection for Him, as would be evident from our sacrifices and our willingness to submit to His holy will.

Mary is our "mystical rose." Under that title she brings to our mind the sweetness and beauty of the life of God in our soul. How good it might be if we journeyed in spirit over to Nazareth, there to inhale the heavenly scent of this finest flower in the nursery of God! Mary could tell us how wonderful is the excursion into the land of the soul, and how audacious its life. As we would look at Mary, she would hardly have to remind us that the joys of a good conscience and of a moral life exceed beyond comparison any other delight on earth. She would tell us of the prickly stems from which the rose is finally born, and would warn us that these stems are precisely why we fail to reach full spiritual stature. Mary knows that we want to love Jesus with the full red color of the rose, but she knows also that we give up too easily in trying to love and to follow Him, when its sharp pointed stems draw a little red blood on ourselves.

Mary would ask us to look beyond the stem and upwards, and see the first bloom of the rose. She would tell us that we have to endure some suffering and sorrow first before we can embrace our Master. She would say that she is the "mystical rose" only because first she was able to say in the words of Jeremias the prophet: "O all ye that pass by the way, attend, and see if there be any sorrow like to my sorrow."

Tower of David

THE CRUSADE FOR THE SALVATION of our immortal soul is the most critical of all battles which we shall ever fight on earth. Other conflicts may seem worse and more distressing. Guns and armaments and hydrogen blasts can take human life easily and in great numbers, but they can never kill the soul nor cause its loss. The soul wings its way to Christ and is judged with a verdict that will last forever.

In this campaign for our soul's salvation we meet with neither the pageantry nor horror ordinarily experienced by men at war. In the constant match between sin and virtue we do not see the glory of the struggle, nor the dull monotony, nor the wounds. We see on one side merely the commandments, while on the other we feel the persuasive, convincing and pleasurable driving force of our lower passions. There is no flourish of trumpets or unfurling of flags, but simply our knowledge of divine rules and, against this, our own craving to satisfy our flesh or pride. And yet on a decision like this rests not the fate of our body, which is lowered into a grave, but the destiny of our soul which could be lowered into hell. In thinking of our own salvation, we should ever be mindful of St. Peter's words concerning the damnation of the evil angels when he wrote in his second letter of the New Testament: "God did not spare the angels when they sinned, but dragged them down by infernal ropes to Tartarus, and delivered them to be tortured and kept in custody for judgment."

Just as on earth men have fought for centuries under the banners of kings and rulers and potentates, so in our struggle to get to heaven, we, too, are enlisted and must fight under the banner of the King of Kings, Jesus Christ. Maybe we are not accustomed to take the field under royal command, but in this matter of our spiritual destiny we have to. Jesus has given us the orders and, as good soldiers, we have no alternative but to obey.

Jesus on earth, even in His humanity, was of royal blood, for He was of the family of King David, one of the most respected and holy kings of God's chosen people. David was the principal author of the Book of Psalms, a poet and a distinguished ruler. As a young boy, David slew the giant Goliath of the Philistines. His name will be remembered among the devout until the end of time. Now Joseph, the foster-father of Jesus, was of the line of David. Even though ancient Jewish genealogical fashion paid no attention to descent from the woman's line, Mary herself was evidently of David's family long before, as even St. Paul attests in his letter to the Romans, when he writes, "Concerning his Son who was born to him according to the flesh of the offspring of David." Bear this in mind as we face the struggle in our lives against temptation. Jesus and Mary and Joseph were of royal blood of the house of King David, and we are spiritually of their same stock.

Mary is called by her Church the "tower of David." She had human regality on earth and, of course, now wears the mantle of royalty in heaven. Her Son's cause on earth was her very life, and now in eternity it is the same, except gloriously more so. Jesus died to save us, and from heaven He will pour forth His aid and His grace upon us as we take up arms to war against the enemies of salvation. But we must remember also that we are enlisted in a campaign to help save not only our own soul, but those of our relatives, friends, acquaintances and even our enemies. We have enrolled beneath a royal insignia in this campaign for souls, and perhaps it is time that we gave serious thought as to how much we are assisting Jesus in His cause, or how little. Have we as yet, by our word or example, led even one soul into Christ's

Church, or one sinner back to the tribunal of Penance?

In the Canticle of Canticles of the Old Testament we read these words, written with regard to the Church, but accommodated to Mary: "How beautiful art thou, my love, how beautiful art thou! . . . Thy neck is as the tower of David, which is built with bulwarks: a thousand bucklers hang upon it, all the armor of valiant men." Perhaps we should take a second look at our life, and for this we might make a visit in spirit to Mary at Nazareth. She would remind us that we are not in this campaign on earth for our own sakes alone, and that, although we have our own soul primarily to save, we have nevertheless an obligation to spread a knowledge of our Faith and to help others attain heaven.

At Nazareth we may discover that we are failing to live up to what Christ expects of us, that we are not doing our part in His campaign on earth for souls. We may find that we are living for ourselves alone, with no sense of obligation toward others and with no consideration of their eternal welfare. From Mary we can learn that this life now takes on in reality the aspect of a great crusade on the part of Christ and His Church to save the souls for whom Jesus died. And that means all men. On our personal support of Christ's campaign will depend our own reward in the next life. And Mary herself will remind us again at

Nazareth of those words from the Canticle of Canticles: "Thy neck is as the tower of David . . . a thousand buckles hang upon it, all the armor of valiant men." When we come to finish our life on earth, shall we be able to hang our shield of battle there as a sign that, for the sake of Jesus, we have been courageous soldiers? After all, nothing else will really count.

Tower of Ivory

In the Canticles of Canticles of the Old Testament we read, in an allegorical description of the beauty of the Church, these words applied to the Blessed Virgin: "Thy neck is as a tower of ivory." And in her litany we hear the Church praying to her under this auspicious name. Ivory has hardness; it is not brittle or weak. Ivory is creamy white in color; debris leaves little stain upon it. Ivory does not reflect or give out light; it stands of itself, solid, endurable and strong. Mary is like ivory. Of all human beings she was morally the strongest, the most pure and chaste, and God has endowed her with such prerogatives and placed such power in her hands that she stands apart by herself in her almost privileged independence in dealing with the souls of men.

Mary is also a tower. Her stature rises from earth to heaven. Raised high to prominence, she can see exactly the will of God from the parapets of her soul and, at the same time, let men and women cross the moat and enter the doors of her tower for protection and succor, for refuge and courage. She then can bring these souls up to the ramparts where they also may see the majesty and the grandeur of God and His will.

Too rarely in life do we reach so high that we can see the will of God with ease and feel affection for it. It is so difficult for us to look upon the Ten Commandments with love, unless deep in our soul we have a profound admiration for God. "I will run in the way of thy commandments," says the Psalmist, "when thou dost enlarge my heart." Jesus, Son of God, is the one who came on earth to proclaim again the commandments of His Father. Now, to cherish these, we must cultivate a very personal relationship with Christ. We must be able to talk with Jesus, as Moses once did with the Almighty Himself when he said, "You have said, 'You are my intimate friend,' and also, 'You have found favor with me.' Now, if I have found favor with you, do let me know your ways so that, in knowing you, I may continue to find favor with you." And it will be Mary of all others who will easily lead us up to the heights of her tower, where we can begin to see things from God's viewpoint instead of always our own.

We are sometimes almost crushed by events in life and circumstances that come upon us. Whether gradual or sudden, they can deal us almost mortal blows from which we may find it hard to recover, unless, of course, we are sheltered by Mary's nearness, and unless we can still see the pure blue of the sky beyond the dark nomadic clouds. Desperate humiliations and hurts, wounded name and reputation, false accusations, misinterpreted motives—all these or any one of them is sufficient to make the strongest among us unnerved, unless we have learned fortunately that God's holy will in action, even in our darkest moments, is the most salutary thing that could happen to us. To absorb this lesson we must stand on the heights with Mary and keep our soul pointed toward the sureness of heaven, not to the ambiguities of earth.

Life can have its shades and shadows, wherein we walk sometimes with grave affliction of heart and numbness of understanding because of the machinations of others. And yet, amid this gloom we must, as Christian followers of Christ, look toward Him on the cross, come close to Him and even embrace Him. We must explore His wounds and come to realize that, compared with Him, we are suffering little. We do however need support in any crisis of this kind, and ordinary help goes only so far. But we can always lean our heart against the "tower of ivory" that is Mary, and she will always respond by coming down and permitting us entrance. She will take us to the far reaches of her tower where the air is clear and from which the world looks so greatly different. The pressure of adversity and the slough of despondency will appear less and not so overwhelming as we look at them from above. Mary will point to heaven where God is and where He rules and reigns, and we shall begin to see how everything that affects us, even with tears, is allowed by God in order that we shall draw closer to Him and become more of a trusted friend.

It would do us a world of good if we undertook a journey to Nazareth and visited the Virgin Mary. If we desire a real personal and intimate feeling for Jesus, then we had better go to His mother first. At home she will not be imposing or awesome as we might suppose a "tower of ivory" would be, but she may impart to our soul some of the qualities for which ivory is known, and she could, as a tower, bring us up above the earth's horizons, there to find a sweeping and more discerning view of the way God's will is at work on earth among us.

Until we come to understand God's will, or until we realize that, no matter what the price we pay, His will must be done, then we shall never find the happiness which we are continually seeking. It is only when it finally dawns on us that God's will, even though it brings us heartache, is the only and the best way for our salvation, that we shall be contented and relieved and glad. For this we need the help of Mary who stands as a "tower of ivory" above the souls of men. She will give us, in a spiritual sense, the tone of ivory, its hardness for the battle against evil, its whiteness for our purity of purpose, and its opaqueness for our durability in life's campaign. Of all these we are in want. So, stay with Mary, and when she introduces Jesus to us again, we shall find an attachment to our Master perhaps unknown before, and one which we may never lose again.

House of Gold

THAT A WOMAN BE CALLED "house of gold" is undoubtedly the finest tribute which can be given
her, and this is what the Church calls our virgin
mother. It is a title at once all-embracing, rich and
comprehensive; and is a sign of the veneration which
Christ's Church has ever shown Mary. In the sound
and flourish of the few short words there is a world
of significance and elegance, too, telling us how
beautiful in the sight of God is the soul of Mary,
and of what moment she is in the plan of the Creator
for all men and women. To be compared to the most
precious metal which the world has, and then to be
termed the very house containing all this wealth, is
evidence of the unworn deference which the Church
has always paid to Mary, and the great and devout
love which the faithful of the Church have contin-
uously had for her. The trophy, "house of gold,"
which Mary carries with her in the litany, expresses

simply, yet with depth, the reverential sentiment which has been universally and always in the Church for this lovely woman and also, at the same time, the precious value she has for our immortal souls.

Gold is the highest form of monetary exchange in the world. It has been used for both good and bad purposes by man. The Ark of the Covenant in the Old Law was made according to these words of God Almighty Himself: "Plate the ark inside and outside with pure gold, and put a molding of gold around the top of it." In the New Testament gold was brought by the Wise Men of the East on their long and, at one time, ticklish trek to Bethlehem. It served as the greatest gift from earthly kings to the new born King from heaven. Yet, on the other hand, because of gold and what it represents, men have through the eras plundered the bodies and the souls of fellow men and women and have even raped the Church of Christ. Murders have been spawned in greed for gold, and so have wars. Lies and grave injustices have followed in its path. Brother has been set against brother, and father against son. Even we ourselves may not have entirely escaped the taint of gold and in our own lives may have sold respect and honor for what its glitter brings. We should be reminded occasionally of what Solomon says in the Book of Ecclesiastes concerning the misery of the covetous man: "The untimely born is better than he. For he came in vain, and goeth to darkness, and his name shall be wholly forgotten. He hath not seen the sun, nor known the distance of good and evil."

There is no doubt that today we are all concerned with money and what it can buy. We have to live with it, and we cannot live without it. It is necessary in order that we sustain and support our families and ourselves. Though many of us are charitable with our possessions, there are those who regard gold as the only means of obtaining security, who become panicky when they think they may be unable to earn it. Gold and the love of gold have an effect upon us which is not always apparent to us. The spirit of mammon can seep through our soul until, all unknowing, we have reached a philosophy of living whereby the spell of gold and what it signifies far outstrip the prominence that belongs to God in our striving. Jesus Himself once said in words we well remember: "If God so clothes the grass which flourishes in the field today but tomorrow is thrown into the oven, how much more you, O you of little faith! Make for yourselves purses that do not grow old, a treasure unfailing in heaven, where neither thief draws near nor moth destroys."

We do have to be conscientious and careful in our attitude toward money. Some of it we may reap unjustly and, though it does afford us a temporary benefit, our conscience will never desist from warning us

144

that some day, before it is too late, a debt must be paid. Or we may have to labor so bitterly and hard for money that we come to look upon it as a sort of god, and then we are in danger that the Almighty in His wrath will destroy the golden calf we have moulded and formed, as He did among the Israelites of old. If there is one spot in our armor where we are vulnerable, it is on this particular question of money, for violations of justice in its regard will open the floodgates to other serious infractions until the whole Ten Commandments come tumbling down.

It would be of much worth to us if in spirit we made a journey to Nazareth. There in the house of Mary we could see the "house of gold." Mary would take us gently by the hand and talk with us. She, who in God's design is the richest of all creatures, would gently caution us against making perishable substances the standard of our living. She would tell us of the night of Epiphany long ago in Bethlehem, when she had both the Christ Child in the manger and the gold of Eastern kings beneath it. Although gold did express in concrete form the generous hearts of Wise Men, it was the Christ whom Mary held in her arms, as she went north again to Nazareth in Galilee, that brought her joy. It certainly was not the gold she held. And we wonder how much, if not all, of that gold was dispersed to the needy along the way back home.

Yes, Mary could easily ask us to take another good look at our spiritual condition to see if we have not bowed to the maxims of the world and its unholy spirit. She would remind us that she herself is the very "house of gold," containing within her soul by God's great decision, not only the abundance of earth, but even the fortune of heaven. She would advise us to watch our heart, lest we hear within the jingle of coins which may be its dearest interest. And then she would repeat the words of her blessed Son which each and every one of us will recall upon our death-bed, either for comfort or distress: "Where your treasure is, there also will your heart be."

Ark of the Covenant

THE MOST SACRED and treasured possession among
the Israelites of old was their "ark of the covenant." The ark was not very large and could be carried. As a matter of fact, it was usually borne into
battle with the army of Israel. The ark was at the
famous siege of Jericho, when the rams' horns blew
and the people shouted and the walls of Jericho came
crumbling down. It was once captured and held for
seven months by their enemies, the Philistines, and
after many decades it was placed in a special tent on
Mt. Sion before the temple of the Jews was built.
The covenant which was within the ark was a book
which contained not only the Ten Commandments
given by God to Moses on Mt. Sinai, but included
also many other ethical and religious laws which God
had prescribed for His chosen people and which were
a very part and parcel of their public and religious
worship. To the Israelites the "ark of the covenant"

147

represented the supreme pact that the Almighty had made with them, and was an ever-living proof that they were a selected nation, designated by God to be entrusted with His revelation and to spread among all men a knowledge of the one true God.

So, it was not just the Ten Commandments which the Israelites were to hold sacred, but many other ordinances as well. Their relationship with their Creator went beyond the realm of the Decalogue, and they were to be bound to God by greater ties even in smaller matters. In thinking of the "ark of the covenant" with Israel, we might reflect in turn upon our own personal attitude toward the commandments. Do we regard them as means of maximum service of the Lord, or of the least service? Well might we revert to the thoughts of the Psalmist concerning the commandments: "Blessed are they . . . who walk in the way of the Lord. Blessed are they who observe his precepts, who seek him with their whole heart, who do no wrong, but walk in his ways. Thou hast given thy precepts to be diligently observed. Would that my way of life were set to observe thy laws! Then I shall not be confounded, when I shall have respect for all thy commandments."

How many of us rest satisfied with a negative approach to God, content that we are not breaking His laws in any serious manner? How few of us, perhaps, rise from the inertness which grips us, and open wide our hearts to let enter in the rays of God's great love? How few of us, perhaps, go out of our way to do anything more than keep the law? This is truly a possible condition on which we might solemnly examine ourselves, for it could be that we may go on through life, observing what we have to, never daring to take a single step forward in giving God something special of ourselves. Besides our few prayers, and the Mass we attend on Sunday, and the charitable contributions which we make, where is the personal effort to know God more, to love Him increasingly each day, and to serve Him as valiant soldiers in His army? Could it not be that we know God less and love Him not so much as we did even a few short years ago? In which direction are we traveling, we who have so many means of love and holiness at our command?

Mary is called by the Church the "ark of the covenant," and of all human beings created she was the most conscious of the majesty of God's will and of the endeavors we must make in order to come to a finer and better understanding of Him. She is the one through whose immaculate frame passed the Son of God. She it was who brought Christ from heaven and gave Him to the sons and daughters of men to cherish, to adore and to serve until the end of time. And today, through Mary, Jesus walks among us as

He did of old in Palestine. Yet, how frequently is He but a stranger in our midst!

The covenant between God and man, though official and public, is a very subjective one as well. It would be good to realize this, for in the process of living we may come to regard our relationship with God as something almost impersonal, an association which in due time can grow cool and even cold. This is why we had better see Mary, for she has the Christ to offer us, Him who is both God and man, and she can very deftly introduce us to Jesus again, for she knows more than we how our intimacy with Him may have gradually declined into a mere acquaintanceship. She will receive us in spirit into her home at Nazareth, and there we can learn as time goes by that Mary possesses an uttermost affection, not only for the commandments as such, but for all those other delicacies of love whereby one can commune more harmoniously and intensely with Jesus who stands ever ready to give His divine Heart in return.

Mary is the "ark of the covenant," and is the most revealing model of a soul who makes overtures of sacred love to her Redeemer. Remaining with her for a time at Nazareth, we shall come to see that perhaps we may be failing in our personal approach to Jesus. If we can give only more of our heart to Christ Jesus, instead of giving Him solely the service of our lips; if we can feel as free with Him as we do with close friends in the world, how much happier we shall be, what stalwart citizens of His kingdom we shall become, and what an asset to Him in His campaign for the souls of men on earth! Then we shall really be living, and in the only way that counts. So, step in spirit over the threshold at Nazareth. There, in the "ark of the covenant" which is Mary, we shall find a new understanding of God's contract with us, and an inspiring motive to give all that we are.

Gate of Heaven

ALL OF US MOST CERTAINLY want to get to heaven after we die. Heaven is our destiny, and it consists in a sharing in the life and happiness of God, of the reward which He has promised us in His contract, if we but serve Him with fidelity on earth. "Amen, amen, I say to you," says Christ Himself, "you shall see heaven opened." It is our only objective which is eternal, the only goal that really counts. Once our body has been lowered into the grave, all the laughter and the loves, all the frowns and the misgivings of this life will be finished forever. The only question of any importance then will be whether we shall spend out eternity with God or apart from Him. Heaven, after all, could be simply another breath away. Regardless of the number of years still left us on this earth, heaven can be rather near, although we may not realize it.

In this life we struggle constantly and to a large

degree for merely human happiness. We frequently receive many setbacks in this quest due to the vagaries and whims of our heart. Even human love receives its share of stir and ferment which dash our hope and disconcert our state of joy. Human love should be the rational and psychic appreciation of another, with the intention of giving more than we receive and of helping the other in his or her frailties and weakness; but how often is its beauty marred by an excess of the physical alone, of trying to inherit much more than we are willing to give and of magnifying after awhile the deficiencies and the fragility of the one we once said we loved. God's life and love and happiness, on the other hand, consist of practically total endowment upon the one He loves, of divine mercy toward any failings, and of endurance that never disappoints.

In the Book of Genesis we read of the vision of Jacob at Bethel, when Jacob fell asleep on the ground and dreamed of the ladder upon which angels were ascending and descending. In his sleep God had appeared to Him and, when he awoke, Jacob said, "Truly the Lord is in this place and I did not know it . . . This is none other than the house of God; this is the gate of heaven." Mary is called "gate of heaven" in her litany. The Church knows that she has so much influence with her Son, Jesus, that she has in her hand all of His mercies for distribution among the daughters and the sons of men. She is the most prevailing with Christ of all His creatures, and in her ascendancy and patronage as His mother, Mary is the very gate through which human souls pass on their way to God, just as she was once, of course, the portal also through which the Son of God came on earth to men. When we think of Mary as the "gate of heaven," we conjure up a vision of everything that Mary is, both to the Church and to ourselves. We are all extremely conscious of this truth, and that is why, in our devotion and our prayer life, it is Mary to whom, more than all other saints, we address our heartfelt and ardent supplications. Deep down within our soul we somehow know that profound devotion to Mary in this life will mean love and life with Mary in eternity.

There are naturally some among us who give but little thought to Mary and the part she plays in our salvation. Some may go along for years without making one novena to this blessed woman. Many, perhaps, never recite the rosary. At our parish mission it is very evident, too, that those who attend the exercises are also they who have a solid devotion to the Blessed Virgin. What they are missing, those who hold not Mary sufficiently in their heart!

It would be good to travel in spirit to Nazareth where, in Mary's home, we shall stay with her who is the "gate of heaven." Soon we shall realize that our expectations concerning heaven may be quite moderate. We think so constantly and wistfully at times about our mortal earthly aims, but perhaps seldom about heaven and the quickness with which it is approaching. Mary may even startle us with the information that up until now we have little chance for heaven because of the way we are living. She will remind us that spiritually we have all that Christ willed us through His Church, even His Body and Blood, but she may gently rebuke us for our procrastination and default.

After we have returned from our visit to Mary, we shall no longer let months and months pass by without receiving the sacraments or miss Mass casually and undisturbed. Predominant in our mind will be the thought of heaven and the seriousness with which we must seek it. So far we may have reflected upon heaven only incidentally and in reverie, but after leaving Mary in Nazareth we shall recognize that the attainment of heaven must be our prime ambition and our chief design for living, and that we had better begin soon to display initiative and effort in our conquest of eternal life.

All we need do is to go to Mary. She will so easily persuade us that so far we may have wasted much of our life in trying to reach ends which today have decayed and died. She will tell us forcefully that we are here on earth for one purpose only, to get to heaven, and that she is the gate through which we must make that journey.

Morning Star

THERE IS PROBABLY NOTHING in all of nature that symbolizes so much the peace and joy of a good conscience as does the morning star. Poised in the sky, distinguished amid the new-born light of early dawn, a star that still retains its strength and far-off beauty after the blackness of the night has been dispelled. In a manner, the morning star signifies the soul that has kept its virtue, or even regained it, after the many hours of temptation through which it may have passed. In looking at the morning star we feel the pure clear breath of dawn, just as in our moral life, if we have not succumbed to what the night can bring, our conscience rests within us, light, clean and comfortably close to God.

The morning star stands watchful like a sentinel over the departing night and the arriving day. It has seen the evil done by men among the shades of night and now it sees the good that will be done by those who early in the morning greet their God. The morning star stands in the sky, observant, bringing together the regrets of the past and the hopes of the future, watching some yield to the magnet of night's lovely hours, seeing others drive away temptation, preferring the fidelity and peace which the morning star augurs.

Mary has been called the "morning star," and we can easily determine the reason why. Our Blessed Lady has first at heart, of course, the interests of Jesus, but she is most solicitous for us as well. Mary realizes what we are experiencing: our struggle to preserve moral rectitude. She is familiar with the magic wand of the spirit of the world and how, with our fallen nature, we are sometimes captivated by it, even conquered. She sees our good intentions, but knows that lower passions often rise and mix with the enchantment of the evening, bringing to us moral languor. She knows too that the dawn will bring, if we have sinned, nothing but dissatisfaction, remorse and blemish of soul. She knows that the price for the pleasures of sin runs high, a price far above what we receive. She is aware that we must face the dawn without embracing it, as we could do if our conscience was clear. The words of Jesus, "I will give him the morning star," contained in St. John's Book of the Apocalypse, are not for the sinner at the dawn.

This is the great conflict in our life, the desire to

bring our soul close to Jesus and the desires which can drag our soul away. The contention will ever go on, but if we wish to ease the strain, then we must make a decision with regard to the "morning star." Shall we be forced to look upon it painfully and distastefully because we sought the luxury and silkiness which the moments of the night have brought, or shall we gaze upon it longingly and expectantly, knowing that we face our God upon another day with breast quite clear of all but love and zeal? Between the two we certainly must choose, between the night of sin and the day of virtue. Both we cannot have, and it is precisely because we sometimes try to achieve the two that we are not the great servants of God we hope to be. It has to be one or the other, for compromise brings only sin. There will always be vacillation and delay, never the giving completely of our heart to Jesus. Yes, we have to look at the "morning star" and choose whether our steps toward Christ be a pursuit of Him or just a groping in the dark, with no real quest at all.

Mary can be to us the "morning star," for our Church prays to her in that way. In the darkness of the night and of temptation we must keep her well in mind, for the day must truly arrive and she will be there, either for our comfort or our distress. We have to choose just how we want to greet her at the dawn, with soul completely hers or with a heart that has been sullied along the way. This is why again we should in spirit go to Nazareth where we can stay with Mary for awhile and learn much more about this "morning star."

At Nazareth we shall be with her who has witnessed above all human creatures both the tragedy of sin and the pricelessness of moral goodness. She has lived on earth as the mother of the Son of God Himself and was wrapped in the divine goodness which is His; but she also has felt acutely the effect of moral evil and knows the warping that takes place in our heart as a result of sin. Mary can tell us much and guide us well on our path to heaven. Gradually she will secure for us the insight and the courage which we need in order to decide just how we shall accept her from now on: as one before whom we never need be embarrassed, or before whom we shall be often ashamed.

Are we not rather abashed to realize that we have any alternative concerning Mary? Are we not taken somewhat aback to know that we may choose our manner of dealing with her? If we have not forsaken Christ through sin, then we can look unafraid upon Mary in the dim morning light; but if we have deserted Jesus, then we must look upon Mary with confusion. At Nazareth she will usurp, and justly so, the words of Jesus which He spoke to St. John in the Book of the Apocalypse: "I am the root and the offspring of David, the bright morning star."

Mary is the "morning star" of our spiritual life, and we had better look toward her in heaven at the start of each day. She will be looking down at us, ready for our glance in her direction. Shall we be able to look her in the face with a smile to match her own? If we can do this every morning, then she will one day change our morning gaze into everlasting life with her in heaven.

Health of the Sick

O NE OF THE PENALTIES which mankind suffered
as the aftermath of the fall of Adam and Eve
is the infirmity of the body and its eventual collapse
and decay. God, when He created, had not intended
this to be, but our first parents' avidity for the contra-
band of Paradise brought on this weakness in our
flesh. So, in consequence, we see sickness not only
among the aged, but at every stage of human life,
even among the very young. From man's first breath
he is subject to disease and, as Hamlet says, "the thousand natural shocks that man is heir to." Yet it is
good to be reminded occasionally that God had never
planned His creatures to be physically ailing, but that
it is man himself who brought it on. That, however,
with which we should be much more concerned is
the health of our soul. So many of us may be spiritually weak when we think we are strong, and, on the
other hand fortunately, many may be well and sound

in soul as they go on humbly believing themselves to be worthless and sinful. These latter are doubtless walking the pathway of the saints.

Tremendous advances have been made in the field of medicine, but what we should realize even more for the sake of our soul, is that the Church for centuries, through its ascetical teaching and the writing of its saints, offers us as individuals every prescription for actual sainthood on earth. Within the Church there is a gold mine of Catholic literature, of knowledge and inspiration, of which we could take such easy advantage; and yet how few of us have ever delved into this treasure which the Church has to offer? The shelves of our Catholic bookstores and information centers are crammed with thousands of books on the Catholic Faith and the spiritual life, but are we able in our own home to find even a single volume?

The truth is that we read all too little of what pertains to our spiritual life or advancement and, as a result, our soul becomes the loser. We are denied the heavenly tonic which can brace up our association with Jesus and strengthen the link of personal affection for Him. Our mind is naturally filled with the phenomenon and excitement of the day, and, unless we take definite means to instill our minds with thoughts of God and of eternal truths, we shall continue through life rather barren of the very impressions that matter. We go to school for many years to study mundane subjects and, at the completion of each semester, we have progressed further in our knowledge. Yet how readily we accept the basic littleness of what we know in the spiritual life and fail to go on any further in the science of the saints.

In the field of education our determination to master a particular thesis or theme shows undoubtedly our intense interest in the topic in question, but the fact that we pay small heed to any continuous exploration of our own spiritual life may betray a lack of any immediate and growing concern over that which is the most commanding and critical alternative of all. In a personal sense, it is sad that we fail to take advantage of the Church's storehouse of spiritual writing, for we shall never know at all the thrilling adventure that lies ahead in the rich realm of the soul.

Mary is called "health of the sick," and we might in a moderate sense affirm that they who fill not their soul with some food for the mind, which the Church so plentifully offers, are not in the best of health at least with regard to an intimate relationship with Jesus. Friendship can suffer much, if the friendship becomes all one-sided. How true for everyone are the words which Jesus at the Last Supper spoke to His Apostles: "You are my friends if you do the things I command you. No longer do I call you servants, because the servant does not know what the master does. But I have called you friends, because all things that I have heard from my Father I have made known to you."

Were we to visit in spirit our Virgin Mother at Nazareth, we might discover that her title, "health of the sick," signifies for us more a vigor and strength of soul than a soundness of body. She will show us her Jesus and remind us again that, before we can ever love and serve Him properly, we must come to know Him much more familiarly than we do. Mary will show us the marked difference between an official acquaintance with Him and a personal love and fervor for Him. And she will ask us, no doubt, to begin grazing upon the language of spiritual writers and of the saints, who long ago have given their mind and heart to Him. She will quote to us these words from the Book of Proverbs: "By instruction the storerooms shall be filled with all precious and most beautiful wealth."

So, make the journey to Nazareth and stay awhile with Mary. Let her tell us, as only she can, how poor we may be in our own spiritual life. She will draw the contrast for us, pointing out how abundantly we may have supplied ourselves with material things, but how bare and empty we may have allowed our soul to become. Mary may even quote the words of Ezechiel the prophet, who writes that God said to him: "Eat this book, and go speak to the children of

Israel." Mary will explain that these words mean the careful attention and affection with which we are to embrace the word of God and the meditation we should make upon it, allowing it to sink within the deep recesses of our soul.

Refuge of Sinners

AMONG ALL THE TITLES which Mary assumes in her litany, the one perhaps by which she is most consoled is that of "refuge of sinners." At the same time we also, being sinful creatures, probably regard Mary more realistically under this aspect than under any other. As human beings subject to life's temptations, succumbing to them sometimes and finding ourselves deprived of Christ's great friendship, we somehow have no hesitancy whatever in going humbly and contritely to Mary first, that she might find again in our behalf forgiveness from the Heart of her Son.

One masterful thing which our Church has accomplished is to keep alive within us a conscience that constantly sounds off the judgment of God. Without a teaching Church and one that has authority we might by now, if left alone unguided and untaught, have gone astray from God's commandments and remained away, with a conscience grown duller and more faint each time we fell from grace. But through the inspiration of our Church, its instruction and its continual reminders of the moral law, we can be grateful that at least we know God's will exactly, that we know what is right and wrong, even though unfortunately we may at times fail through weakness. We mention weakness rather than malice, for it is more the one who sins through frailty who returns to Jesus through Mary than it is the sinner who defects through spite and rancor.

"Refuge of sinners!" We have known Mary under this name since our youthful days. As we grew older and tasted for the first time of sin and its bitterness, we may have been afraid to approach Jesus in the confessional. Of course it was Mary to whom we prayed for courage, who gently reassured us, and who led us to the tribunal of mercy where in gratitude we left our tears. And then life went on, and kept going on, and it may be that many times we slipped away again from the grace of Christ. Embarrassed and remorseful, sorry that we had hurt Jesus, again and again we went back to the judgment seat of confession, buoyed up and helped on by the calming and never-failing touch of Mary.

Truly Mary is the "refuge of sinners," and it is under this designation that each of us personally is best familiar with her. No doubt all of us try to love

Jesus and serve Him. None of us has any intention of hurting Him, but passion sometimes hits us hard, or sloth or gluttony, and we feel as outcasts from the living God. We feel almost as did Adam when, as we read in the Book of Genesis, "The Lord God put him out of the garden of Eden . . . He drove out the man." Then suddenly there is Mary who, as she once did at Cana, says to us, "Do whatever he tells you." Under her tender persuasion and heartening encouragement, we follow her counsel and we are in the arms of Jesus once again.

Of course, in all this going and coming to the confessional, in our struggle to maintain integrity with the Lord, we must keep in mind that our object must be the eventual conquest of even our sins of weakness. We have to plan and take precaution often to avoid the pitfalls into which we have been so apt to fall. Weakness can be built with God's good grace into a strength which is quite surprising, and Isaias the prophet says, "It is the Lord that giveth strength to the weary, and increaseth force and might to them that are not." It is in this feature of supernatural sorrow that Mary's interest, as "refuge of sinners," would lie, that we by valiant effort and concerted plan draw closer in personal affection for Jesus and eliminate along the way the errors and the rifts of our lives.

True, Mary is the sanctuary to which we can repair when sin has blurred our vision and turned our heart. She knows that we are children of Adam and Eve, exposed to much temptation from all sides, and when we seek her as a haven in order to drop our tears and regain her love, Mary embraces us with open arms and comforting heart, conscious that she is mankind's "solitary hope," and that she is the easiest way to the Heart of Jesus. Mary knows the mercy of the Son of God. She witnessed it so often during His life on earth. She remembers the day when Peter came up to Our Lord and asked, "How often shall my brother sin against me, and I forgive him? Up to seven times?" And Mary remembers the answer of Jesus: "I do not say to thee seven times, but seventy times seven." This naturally is an indefinite number, and simply means that a sinner should be forgiven as often as he repents. On the other hand, even "seventy times seven" has some sort of conceivable limit, and it is this limit toward which Mary looks, and on which she centers her hopes concerning us. She wants us sometime to return to Jesus completely and with all our heart.

Go over in spirit to Nazareth and dwell for awhile with this first lady of God. We shall feel her immaculate presence and inhale the very fragrance of heaven. As sinners, we shall find our refuge, where we can be free again and our soul made clean, where we shall learn that nothing can compare to the joy of a virtuous heart, and where we may actually come to decide never to leave the Lord our God another time. The sooner we do, the better. Then we shall begin to live more adventurously than ever before, and we shall realize that all our daring up till now in the escapades of earth has been as nothing in comparison with our enterprises on the road to God. Mary is the "refuge of sinners," primarily to turn our hearts that other way.

Comforter of the Afflicted

IN SO MANY WAYS we are disturbed in life, per-
plexed, confused and saddened. Misunderstanding
may make heavy our heart, or humiliation or false
accusation, and these afflictions of soul we feel more
than those of flesh. Physical pain we can understand,
even if sometimes we cannot grasp why it should
come to us; but blight of a soul is a more serious
affair, one which leaves us limp, perhaps, or empty,
cold and lonely. We are dejected at the quick turn
of events that have cost us a friend or that have
placed blame upon our shoulders undeservedly. We
feel helpless somewhat in trying to redeem a reputation, and are thrown back on our own resources
when sometimes there are none. We are left with
no chance to explain, or the interpretation will serve
only to deepen the trouble, and so we find at times
drawn away from us a heart whose love once brought

172

us warmth and understanding. Now it is gone, and we are alone.

The only real way to accept these unfortunate turns of circumstance is to regard them as portions of the cross which Jesus sends to us, asking us to share His pain. Perhaps He sees us quite forgetful of Him amid all our loves and pastimes in the world, and through these twistings of our hopes and dreams wants to make us see that He as well could possibly be lonesome for our love. A startling fact which underlies such trials of soul is that in willingly acceding to them, even though our feelings cry out much in protest, we can surprisingly become rather pleasantly resigned and peaceful. We say "surprisingly" because seldom, perhaps, have we ever tried to look upon these crises as invitations from Jesus to the cross. We generally attempt to fight them off as best we can, and sometimes do rash things and even become bitter; but if we honestly looked at Christ and realized that He wants us very near Him, then should we know the reason for the kind of cross He sends. We might even begin to understand that only a particular affliction will serve, if we accept it properly, to draw us near Him.

We do have to be realistic about these things, and often we are not. We have to learn sometime that tribulations of soul are as much a part of life as the glories. The more quickly we comprehend this, the

173

happier servants of Christ shall we be. Subjecting ourselves graciously and generously to the cross of sorrow, and to the one especially that Christ may send, will not come to us in a day, and maybe not for a long time, but it must come if we are to live a genuine Christian life. We need help for the bearing of these burdens, and no one could possibly assist us more ably or inspire us more zealously than our dear Virgin Mother whom the Church calls officially "comforter of the afflicted."

Mary has been through all grief and mental suffering on earth. Nearest and dearest to Jesus of everyone in the world, she endured more anguish and agony than any other human being has or ever will. Simeon in the temple was correct when he prophesied that her "own soul a sword shall pierce." From the Gospel accounts one would hardly know that Mary went through torment and distress; nevertheless on Calvary Mary's soul was transfixed because of the crucifixion of her innocent Son, and even this was but the end of many months of trembling and anxiety in His behalf. Misunderstanding and mistake came to Mary not long after Annunciation Day. St. Matthew tells us in his Gospel that "when Mary his mother had been betrothed to Joseph, before they came together, she was found to be with child by the Holy Spirit. But Joseph her husband, being a just man, and not wishing to expose her to reproach, was minded to put her away privately." What embarrassment and humiliation for her who was then bearing within her womb the unborn Redeemer of mankind! This was only the beginning of Mary's desolation which would run so consistently through her life until she reached martyrdom itself in her soul, and resembled then quite closely the shorn lamb who was her Son.

Most certainly our Virgin Mother qualifies completely as "comforter of the afflicted." With all the suffering in spirit which we meet in life, and which is much more grievous than physical pain, there is no one better to whom we may go for comfort and assuagement than Mary herself. When we feel lonely and unwanted, or are blamed for things we never did, or hurt by jealous hearts, then Mary is the one whom we should seek. And this is why we must go over in spirit to Nazareth where the Virgin lives, and rest in her home for awhile. The bitterness, the envy and the tears which we might carry with us there will all be washed away by Mary's smile. Her words to us will take away the load upon our heart. If we can but learn to receive the cross with holy resignation—which we shall learn to do if we let Mary be our guide—then shall we find that the burden which we thought so heavy is no longer there. Mary has simply transferred the weight of the cross to her Son who once said, "My yoke is easy, and my burden light."

175

Yes, Jesus will bear the pressure of the very cross He gives us, but only if we are actually willing to share His pain. Mary at Nazareth could help us to accept tribulation with perhaps even a tiny touch of cheerfulness, and, if we ever come to that, then we shall have advanced much on the road to a full Christian life. There is just one other thought. By going to Mary at Nazareth, we ourselves may even comfort her. How wonderful it would be to make up for the lonely nights she must have spent on earth, wondering what pain and evil men would next bring to her beloved Son!

Help of Christians

As Christians who are trying to follow Christ, we have a vocation to answer and a mission to perform. Just because we have been gifted with our precious Faith, we cannot rest upon any presumptive laurels, for, as far as our Faith is concerned, we actually have not won any trophy or ribbons as yet. We have to realize that Christ Jesus wants all men to be saved, even our personal enemies and those who despise our Church. Christ suffered and died for every one, and we must begin to understand that God has given us our Faith in order to aid Jesus in His work of converting souls. Consequently we have a moral obligation to spread the knowledge of our Faith among mankind. And on this duty it would be well occasionally to examine ourselves.

So often our considerations of Catholicism are limited to our own small sphere. It is true that we give generously to the missions both at home and abroad, and that we support well the various charities of the universal Church when appeals are made, to say nothing of our own parish support; but we have to beware lest we confuse the giving of what we have, with what would be even more acceptable to God, and that is, the giving of what we are. When we are beset by many intricacies in family life or in business affairs, our prayers to the good God are mostly for the solution of our own personal problems. But because we have the charge ever upon us of helping Jesus to convert all men, then we must be generous in prayer at all times and, besides praying for our own wishes and desires, include regularly in our prayer life the great plans and projects which God has for the souls of men and women. God has so many things in mind for our own profit and for the benefit of the Church, but He wants us to ask Him personally in these matters, and frequently He awaits the achievement of His designs until He hears our petitions and our overtures.

We have a big task ahead of us. Priests are conscious of the work to be done for Christ because they have been divinely commissioned, but our people may not think very often of the concern which they too must have in the affairs of Jesus. True, so many of them are apostolic in their thinking and in their undertakings, but the great multitude of Catholics are rather removed from the battle line in the Church's warfare against evil and error. Not that our

178

people are reluctant to help, but they feel preponderantly unable to cope with the intellectual and moral evils of the day; in a way they are forced to leave the struggle in the hands of the clergy or of those trained for the campaign.

The Blessed Virgin Mary is officially called "help of Christians" by the Church, and this title is rather inclusive. Christians, as we know, are all they who wish and profess to follow Jesus, even though we do believe that an enormous number of Christians have been led into error concerning the teachings of Christ on the moral law and on eternal truth. The great body of Christians whom we call non-Catholic are to a great extent a devout people who want to love Christ and serve Him, but we feel that their correct knowledge of Him has been betrayed. In their bloodstreams runs the ancient remnant of the Catholic Faith, although their heritage by now is thoroughly Protestant. Mary must look down to them from heaven with love but with regret, for possibly nothing is dearer to her immaculate heart than that they return to the true Faith of her divine Son. But are her prayers for them and the official prayers of our Church the only ones that reach the throne of God in their behalf? Could it possibly be that the Holy Spirit, before He would illumine their minds and draw their hearts from error, is waiting for the com-

179

bined recurrent prayers of each of us for their conversion?

This is indeed something of which we should be very conscious. Of course we have our own problems and difficulties and at times they do seem immense, but, on the other hand, the return of the non-Catholic world to the true Faith is probably of much more serious consequence with Christ. "Go rather to the lost sheep of the house of Israel," He once said to His Apostles, and with these words we can read Christ's Heart somewhat. On another occasion to those who were following after Him, He stated, "I was not sent except to the lost sheep of the house of Israel." And who can ever forget these poignant words of Christ?: "I am the good shepherd, and I know mine and mine know me . . . And other sheep I have that are not of this fold. Them also I must bring, and they shall hear my voice, and there shall be one fold and one shepherd." Yes, it is easy to see what takes prominence in Christ's mind, and because of this we should be more aware of the issue.

Let us go to Nazareth and see Mary for awhile. She knows the Heart of Christ and His desires. She knows how ardently He seeks the turn of the tide with the non-Catholic world. Mary would inform us perhaps of the fact that Jesus may not make much of a gesture for their return until all of us who have the Faith, personally and privately begin to bombard heaven with our prayers. Mary would remind us of our mission and our vocation, which is to convert the world. She realizes that we have many tears of our own to shed, but she could tell us that some of the tears which Jesus once let flow, were for those perhaps who walked away from Him and stayed away. Mary might call to our attention also that she is the "help of Christians," not just Catholics.

Queen of Angels

BELIEF IN THE EXISTENCE of the angels is a true heritage of our Catholic Faith. Fortunately, along the trail of history, we did not let their memory fade into oblivion, but with our Church we kept our belief in them so that today, even though we be grown men and women, mature and intelligent, we can still pray to the angels as simply as would a child in his own little way. Perhaps as adults we do not converse with them as often as we should, or even think of them enough, but at least we know that the angels are there, the good in heaven and the evil ones in hell. After all, it was for the bad angels first that hell was created. St. Peter himself, in his second letter in the New Testament, says, "God did not spare the angels when they sinned, but dragged them down by infernal ropes to Tartarus, and delivered them to be tortured and kept in custody for judgment."

As we reflect upon the angels and their destiny, we are forced to think of ourselves in almost the same way. Theirs was a sublime creation, the first products of God's overflowing love, but theirs also was a swift judgment, with never a chance for the bad angels to repent, no matter what their rank or dignity or power was. Our destiny, of course, is exactly the same, heaven or hell. True, we have time now, given to us by the Almighty, to prove how greatly we could love Him, but time runs short for every one of us, and at the very end our judgment will of necessity also be either heaven or hell. The sole difference between the angels and ourselves, as far as the testing is concerned, is that we are now being given an allotted number of years in which to make ready for heaven. We have many opportunities for repentance and for acts of charity. When the angels sinned through pride, they had no other chance.

Of all the messages that angels have delivered to this earth from God, none is more memorable than that of the Archangel Gabriel, when he appeared on Annunciation Day to the Blessed Virgin Mary and said to her, "Hail, full of grace, the Lord is with thee. Blessed art thou among women." Then, to make most evident the reason for his coming, Gabriel said to the young woman who would some day be his queen, "Do not be afraid, Mary, for thou hast found grace with God. Behold thou shalt conceive in thy womb and shalt bring forth a son; and thou shalt call his name Jesus." Of all the many times recorded in Holy Scripture that angels have served as emissaries from God to man, the one occasion most associated in our mind is this one, and it concerns the Blessed Virgin Mary.

In that tremendous moment when heaven delivered its gracious ultimatum to earth through Mary that a Redeemer was to begin His coming, it was an archangel who carried the message from God the Father. God Himself did not tell Mary directly but chose instead one of His own angelic creatures, to bring this news which was the finest the world will ever hear. Because of this event alone, we must be intently mindful of the caliber of the good angels as well as of their paramount standing with God, and we in turn should raise our minds to them more often, knowing that it is our own immortal soul which causes us to resemble them, and realizing further that our own spiritual life should be like that of theirs, both in our adoration of the great God now and in the ceaseless quest of our own eternal destiny. The Psalmist says that God "hast made man a little less than the angels." Notice, only "a little less"! Naturally then, we might reflect upon these sacred creatures of God, and try to imitate them in the worship and the praise which endlessly they pay to their Creator. As a practical means of echoing the reverence and laud given by the angels to God, we might slowly revise our own attitude toward Mass, asking ourselves seriously if we approach the Sacrifice as we ought, with a spirit of meditation and the acclaim of a silent heart. Too often we may be at holy Mass with the phantoms of the world still running riot in our imagination and the affections of our nature diverted far from the Body and Blood of Christ upon the altar. How do the unseen angels act who fill the sanctuary during Mass, and how do we?

Mary is called by the Church the very "queen of angels." She stands above these first glorious creatures of a loving God. Though Mary on earth was but a human person, she has been raised by the Almighty to a height beyond them, elevated as their queen, and the good angels who constantly sing forth God's praise in heaven at the same time salute Mary as the one to whom their own angelic loyalty is also pledged. We should in many ways act as the angels do now, for they at present perform and enjoy the very things we too will delight in and do on some glorious and eternal day. True, we cannot look at angels, and it may be difficult for us to imagine their holiness and happiness, but we are destined for this same reward, and to emulate them we might more easily go to Mary as their queen.

Mary is the confidante of angels. She was such on earth with Gabriel and with angels who once sang

on the first Christmas night. She must be more intimate with them in the courts of the eternal God. We
too have been ordained for everlasting happiness and
holiness. Even in this life our major aim is happiness.
The mistake we frequently make is trying to be
happy without being holy. Mary would clear away
this derangement for us. A short journey in spirit to
Nazareth, where we could stay for a while with her,
would result in a revelation from Mary's own lips on
how we might obtain the very thing we so much seek
in life, but which up until now we may have been
seeking so blindly.

Queen of Patriarchs

THE CATHOLIC CHURCH is an ancient Church, even if we go back only to the first Pentecost Day, when the Church was born and infused with the divine life of God the Holy Spirit. But our Church in its human roots peers deeply into the recesses of the Old Testament, where amid Hebrew laws and traditions, culture and a knowledge of the one true God, preparations were being made by the Almighty for the "fullness of time," when the Son of God Himself would sojourn upon earth. The Church today in a certain sense can be seen far back in the days of the patriarchs, whose authority from God over the Hebrew nation embraced the family, the Church and the State. The patriarchs were the Hebrew men of almost dateless and ancestral days whom God raised up among the people to found tribes and clans, to represent the Almighty in their stead, and to rule them by the laws and decrees propounded to them by the Creator Himself. They were the guiding hand to the Hebrews with whom God had made a contract and to whom He had entrusted His revelation. They lived an extremely long time on earth, performed their appointed tasks ably and well, and then, as the Old Testament simply relates, they died.

The patriarchs are a living proof of the length of time God has been interestedly dealing with the human race. They are the human voice of the Almighty, resounding in the primal niches of recorded time, leaders and teachers and escorts of God's chosen people. Adam and Lamech and Noe his son, Sem, Eber and Phaleg; then those with whom we are more familiar: Abraham and Isaac and Jacob, Juda and Levi and the other sons of Jacob, and the heads of the twelve tribes—these were the patriarchs selected by God to rule, to guard and to direct His people.

Of course, living in this age of nuclear weapons, in this day when man-invented satellites are whirling around the earth, our thoughts are not very much on patriarchal eras, nor are they expected to be. Nevertheless, it scarcely escapes the mind of any one of us that what man has with his skill devised, and what could be used so wonderfully for peace, may ultimately be used for war with all its devastation. This could well mean the end of earthly living, the end of the world, and by the ill use of the implements of horror which are now at his disposal man himself

188

might possibly bring about a fulfillment of these words of Jesus: "There will be signs in the sun and moon and stars, and upon the earth distress of nations bewildered by the roaring of sea and waves; men fainting for fear and for expectation of the things that are coming on the world; for the powers of heaven will be shaken." Even then nothing else will matter except the salvation of our soul, and Jesus goes on to say, "Take heed to yourselves, lest your hearts be overburdened with self-indulgence and drunkenness and the cares of this life, and that day come upon you suddenly as a snare. For come it will upon all who dwell on the face of all the earth."

The patriarchs may seem to us as great men, true, but men who lived in a dreamy long-ago. Yet the principles for which they stood in that era of antiquity are the same convictions for which we must strive in our own lives today, believing strongly in the word of God, fearlessly speaking it forth, and courageously living in its behalf. If we do just that in fighting for our soul's salvation, then we are linked closely with the holy patriarchs of the past, who in heaven are glorious and immortal and who have been so since Christ died on the cross. The patriarchs were the first chosen ones of God, and we who read these words are but the last so far, with heaven the common aim.

Mary is called by the Church "queen of patriarchs." She reigns even over them, and yet in the process of time she came not until centuries later. However, in the Book of Ecclesiasticus these words that were written concerning the gift of wisdom have been applied by the Church to Mary: "I came out of the mouth of the Most High, the firstborn before all creatures . . . And I have stood in all the earth; and in every people, and in every nation I have had the chief rule . . . From the beginning, and before the world, was I created." Yes, Mary is truly the "queen of patriarchs," for although they served their God with fidelity and loyalty and care, Mary is the one through whom the Son of God moved in among the children of earth. She was His very mother, and her precedence in heavenly processions is unquestioned.

The fact, however, is that, despite all our modern and exciting way of living, we still have one primary goal, to earn heaven by our morally good life on earth. It may seem drab, this constant faithfulness to the commandments, especially against the scintillating stimulation which our present age offers. Trips to the moon no longer strain imagination, but our journey to heaven at the end of time is all that really counts.

So hurry over to Nazareth for a visit with Mary. Amid the drama of our time, its provocation and commotion, stay with Mary for a while and be at rest. As "queen of patriarchs" she knows both the old and the new. Mary will show us how even we, small though our influence be, can imitate the patriarchs whose lives were spent for others and dedicated to the service of God. Perhaps up until now we have been living for ourselves, expecting all the while that God must serve us.

Queen of Prophets

THE PROPHETS OF the Old Testament are in a sense familiar to the Catholic mind, but perhaps in no such manner or degree as they ought to be. From time to time in the liturgical prayers of the Church we hear their names mentioned, and in that way we know of them; but our acquaintance with these holy men is rather slight. The prophets were remarkable men of the ancient past, selected and inspired by God, whose minds He illumined and whose wills He reached, enabling them to proclaim what He dictated to them from within. God also made known His will to the prophets by dreams and sometimes by visions in the night. How important the prophets should and could be in our lives is brought home to us by Jesus Himself when, in appearing after His resurrection to the two disciples on the road to Emmaus, He exclaimed, "O foolish ones and slow of heart to believe in all that the prophets have spoken!"

192

And at almost the beginning of His public life Jesus with a stern reminder says, "Do not think that I have come to destroy the law or the prophets. I have not come to destroy, but to fulfill."

Of the so-called "sixteen prophets," though there are actually more, four are called the "greater": Isaias, Jeremias, Ezechiel and Daniel. These are not exactly strangers to us, and we know them more than we do the other twelve, or "lesser," prophets: Osse, Joel, Amos, Abdias, Jonas, Micheas, Nahum, Habacuc, Sophonias, Aggeus, Zacharias and Malachias. Micheas is the one who wrote those beautiful words so long in advance of the birth of Christ: "And thou, Bethlehem Ephrata, art a little one among the thousands of Juda: out of thee shall he come forth unto me that is to be the ruler in Israel."

The prophets, as their name implies, foretold future events for the Hebrew people. Then, when a prophecy came to pass and people of a later date saw the culmination of it, their faith in the one true God naturally increased, and the bond between Israel and the Almighty was further cemented. God loved His chosen ones, but they were subject to trial and error. Often they even ran away from God and were unfaithful. They adored false idols. God had to keep His mighty hand upon them, and the prophets were His choice to preserve the Hebrews in their faithfulness, to keep their hearts upon eternity and

193

not on earth, and to guarantee that the old covenant was kept. Jeremias himself reminds us of the significance of the prophets when he wrote that the Lord came to him, saying, "Before I found thee in the bowels of thy mother, I knew thee; and before thou camest forth out of the womb, I sanctified thee, and made thee a prophet unto the nations." So the prophets are of valuable interest in our spiritual life. Their message is aimed at us as well. Through Old Testament history we see them all pointing toward the greatest Prophet of all, Jesus Christ, who would be Redeemer too, and finally Judge. St. John the Baptist in the desert of Judæa, crying out to the people to repent, says of Jesus, "This is he who was spoken of through Isaias the prophet . . . He will baptize you with the Holy Spirit and with fire. His winnowing fan is in his hand, and he will thoroughly clean out his threshing floor, and will gather his wheat into the barn; but the chaff he will burn up with unquenchable fire."

We have been well warned that Jesus does not want to have come to earth, for the salvation of our souls, in vain. He suffered and died that we might be saved; He has left His Sacramental Presence with us from the day of our First Communion. He does not want to lose us and His love for us is infinite, but He knows that such can happen, that we can in a crisis in life walk out on Him, maybe never to return in time. He has forewarned us of the possibility of hell, if we persist in evading and avoiding Him. Because the spirit of the world is so pleasantly contagious and influential on our fallen nature, because of the loneliness and the lonesomeness of our human hearts (because we have not learned to love our Master as we should, or love other persons more), we are liable to go off in a time of scorching trial or hard dilemma toward the wrong direction, never to retread our footsteps toward Jesus. Heed the voice of the prophets while there is yet time. Their voice rings out from long ago, down through the ages, even until this day. Jeremias writes that God said, "I have sent to you all my servants, the prophets, from day to day, rising up early and sending."

Mary is the "queen of prophets." Perhaps we have only a faint idea that the words of the prophets are addressed to us. Perhaps we feel the prophets are oldfashioned, meant for a people of another day. Mary is their queen, and good it would be to journey in spirit to Nazareth, where we could stay with Mary and ask her about these fearless men of old. Mary would remind us of her own prophetical words in her Magnificat: "Behold, henceforth all generations shall call me blessed." But she would not stop there. She would recall to us Lourdes and Fatima, where she appeared from heaven, warning us to do penance. She would make us aware of the significance of the prophets in our own life and, by her gracious presence but unfeigned words, would tell us frankly that, to save our souls and to live quickly with Jesus and herself forever when we die, we had better change our lives and act not only as penitents in the sight of Christ, but criminals as well. For are we not just that?

Queen of Apostles

TRULY, the Blessed Virgin Mary was never more a queen to any group of persons on earth than she was to the Apostles in their arduous and vast struggle to absorb themselves the teachings of Christ, and then later to strike and impress with those doctrines the minds and hearts of all who lived in their time. In their training to convert the world Christ once spoke to them in chilling words: "Behold, I am sending you forth like sheep in the midst of wolves. Be therefore wise as serpents, and guileless as doves. But beware of men; for they will deliver you up to councils, and scourge you in their synagogues, and you will be brought before governors and kings for my sake, for a witness to them and to the Gentiles." Hardly is there need to say that, on an occasion such as this, fainthearted Apostles went hurriedly to Mary's home where they could sit about with her

and listen to her graceful words. She rallied their
fallen spirits, heartened and reassured them.

The Apostles needed a lady, and Mary was given
to them. In those dismal days before the coming of
the Holy Spirit, in the darkened hours of Christ's
passion and His death, Mary was not far from them.
They needed her womanly heart, whose affection for
them was equal in a certain sense to the love she had
toward her own Son. They required her silent courage and her valiant heart. They had to hear from her
own lips the reserved expressions that would make
them understand and accept the fact that their priesthood would consist primarily in their own identifi-
cation with their Master on the cross. Elation which
Bethlehem had brought to Mary herself and the mag-
nificence which some Apostles had witnessed on Tha-
bor were now over. The priesthood loomed ahead,
with its living and dying for Jesus, and that meant
a cross resembling in some terrifying aspects the
crucifixion and the death of Jesus on Calvary. Yes,
the Apostles needed Mary, required her more than
any one but Christ Himself, for they looked into a
future which offered them externally only a little of
joy and a token of glory, but which beckoned them
really to the keen sharp edge of a sword.

To look upon the cross of Christ and to comprehend that it was meant for them besides, would of itself have betrayed the Apostles into the weak human

persons they were, for they remembered that Jesus once had said, "You will be hated by all for my name's sake . . . No disciple is above his teacher, nor is the servant above his master . . . He who does not take up his cross and follow me is not worthy of me." The Apostles knew their own weaknesses, their fears, and how they might individually fail in one respect or another, but Mary was always at their side when the fierce conflict within them grew, and she must have reminded them of Christ's words over Lazarus, "This sickness is not unto death, but for the glory of God, that through it the Son of God might be glorified." This, then, was the first purpose of the priesthood, God and His glory, no matter what embarrassment or humiliation the individual Apostle might have to suffer. And the other purpose—what was it? Mary recalled for them Jesus' own words: "I lay down my life for my sheep. And other sheep I have that are not of this fold. Them also I must bring, and they shall hear my voice, and there shall be one fold and one shepherd." The price would be high for each Apostle, persecution and harassment from the outside, or perhaps a baffling and inglorious failing from within.

Mary was not only the woman with whom the Apostles would share their love and their companionship; she was their queen, to whom they would pledge their loyalty and very lives. She would give them counsel; they would give her the knowledge of a human priestly heart. She would give them fortitude; they in return would promise to follow her Son down into the grave. She would tell them of the Holy Spirit whom she knew; they would await His coming on Pentecost Day, even though they huddled near her during the long ten days of waiting. Mary was to be the center of their hopes and dreams, even after Pentecost, when fearlessly they waded forth into the lives of men and women, into a world of love and hate. Daringly they spoke for Jesus and suffered hard for Him. They still were human souls, although touched by God the Holy Spirit, and in their humanity they came back to Mary often, to breathe the heavenly essence of her, to renew their troth, and to feel again the touch of her delicate hand upon their shoulders, which fashioned them as knights in the service of their queen.

Mary is the "queen of Apostles," but she is queen to all men and women who love her and follow her. To say that we love her is sometimes just a statement. But to follow her, to pursue her through the travail of life, to walk down into "a dark valley," as the Psalmist says, is quite another story. We do not want the particular crosses which Christ sends us, and sometimes we are forced almost against our will to carry them upon our breaking backs and hearts. Go over to Nazareth in spirit for a while, and let Mary again tell us that the reason for our own cross is the glory of God and the salvation of souls, especially and most graphically the salvation of our own. The Psalmist says, "The Lord takes me along paths that are straight for his name's sake." Walking a straight path is oftentimes most hard. Mary can gradually make it so easy.

Queen of Martyrs

"HE WHO WOULD SAVE his life will lose it; but he who loses his life for my sake and for the gospel's sake will save it." These paradoxical words were spoken by Jesus to His own disciples and to the crowd who one day came out to hear Him in one of the villages of Cæsarea Philipi. This statement, strangely enough, expresses concisely the essence of the true Christian's life. We say "strange," because all of us want dearly to continue living, want to hold on desperately to life as long as we can, and we do dread dying. Yet Jesus tells us that only by yielding our memory and freedom for His sake while on earth will we live in heaven eternally, and also that if we live only for this world and its ambitions, refusing to offer Him our mind and will while here, we can definitely lose heaven forever.

Whenever we think of the long list of martyrs, of the intrepid men and women who ever since the

Church was born have laid down their lives for the sake of Jesus and His teachings, we are generally confronted with perplexing thoughts. We esteem and most certainly honor them. This we cannot help but do. We admire them from afar. Then we think of the sword and the stoning and the branding with fire, and we wonder if we could ever be so valiant. The martyrs were human beings like ourselves, afraid of pain and torture and the rack. God's grace was with them certainly when they came to die, but we still wonder if we could possibly be that brave.

Jesus once said to those who followed Him, "If anyone wishes to come after me, let him deny himself, and take up his cross, and follow me." Not all of us can die in the instant a martyr's death. Probably none of us will be asked to give our life for Christ, as did the many martyrs. But martyrdom does not consist in dying for Christ only by physical flame or crucifixion or a rapier's thrust. Martyrdom actually can take a long time. Christ once said, "From the days of John the Baptist until now the kingdom of heaven has been enduring violent assault, and the violent have been seizing it by force."

It takes much struggle and a courageous heart to battle through the storm clouds of this life and to attain heaven in the end. The way is marked for every one of us with difficulties that seem sometimes insurmountable. Some must suffer in sickness of

203

body; many more must suffer sorrow of soul. There is the ache of a mother's heart of a wayward son, the pangs of a wifely heart for a husband who has lost his love and her respect. There is the blow of a daughter's child born out of wedlock, the agonizing helplessness toward a friend who has been guilty of betrayal.

Where once the skies were a soft blue, and the sun up above a warming sphere, when life was gay and unperturbed, when we could look forward to a future of joy, life was an exhilarating thing. But suddenly and so often undeservedly the sky turns dark, and the rays of the sun are removed; the earth is cold, and the rains come driving down upon the human heart, smashing apart all bold visions that once we may have had, leaving us humiliated and crushed and tearful beneath the impact of a mighty lashing. But this is life, the other is not, and it is then we are reminded again of those words of Christ: "If anyone wishes to come after me . . . let him take up his cross." It may seem to us that we can never bear the particular cross which He sends, that we will be mashed under its oppressive load. We are tempted to give up the fight, to scream aloud against our God, even to leave Him. There is the beginning of martyrdom, if we but hold on willingly, and it may last for a long, long time. What about the Apostle John who became a martyr by exile, but a martyr just the same?

What about Mary whose martyrdom was a crucifixion totally in her soul? St. Paul consoles us, however, with these words to the Corinthians: "God is faithful and will not permit you to be tempted beyond your strength, but with the temptation will also give you a way out that you may be able to bear it."

Even with these comforting words our trial may cause us to be bitter. Human nature cries out for assuagement when it has been brutally hurt. We may go off on the wrong road, tossing reason and common sense aside, aiding and abetting some inherent weakness of our own, making it harder all the while to regain stability and to return to the Master. This is when we do need Mary, and much more than we may realize. This is why we should repair in spirit to her home in Nazareth, where we might listen again to the words of Jeremias the prophet, placed by the Church on Mary's lips: "O all ye that pass by the way, attend, and see if there be any sorrow like to my sorrow."

No matter what we have to endure, no matter what our cross may be, whether it come from others or from a delicate but slavish weakness of our own, our distress will never equal Mary's. Mary is called "queen of martyrs," and do not think that the title is simply a term of honor. It is much more than that, for Mary earned that distinction in a terribly hard way. At Nazareth we would marvel at the fair loveliness of her, but beneath that gracious front would be a soul, a soul more beautiful, of course, than that of any creature, but a soul marked and scarred by agony and scourging and a crowning with thorns, by the humble carrying of a cross and finally crucifixion. But look where she is today, the crested glory of heaven, the very queen of martyrs! We shall be with her soon, if we can only bear that cross!

Queen of Confessors

SHINING TODAY AS JEWELS in the diadem of heaven, sharing in a glorious reward for their fearless loyalty on earth to Jesus Christ, are an abundant host of souls whom the Church calls confessors. They were once the great bishops and priests of the Church who, although not asked to shed their blood for Christ, nevertheless devoted earnestly and zealously every faculty in their possession in heroic testimony to the Faith. Long ago the martyrs were called confessors, but in modern terminology these are in a class apart. Today those are known as confessors who were not martyrs in the strict sense, but men who while alive gave their minds and hearts and souls to Jesus, to His Church and to its teachings. They are heroes without the spilling of blood.

While we note this distinction, we might try to discover if in any positive way we are emulating these saintly confessors. We are members of the same

Church as they; we accept the same authority and believe in identical doctrines. We have the Mass which they celebrated, the seven sacraments which they administered. But have we any of their eagerness and ardor to help spread the Faith? There are those not of the fold who perhaps are weeping in their secret hearts, especially in this day of the approaching whirlwind, for truth and guidance and infallible instruction. What an opportunity we have by example, prayer and sacrifice to absorb the fervor of the confessors, so that we too might lead a sinner from his wayward path! Remember the words of Jesus to His Apostles, and to us as well: "Everyone who acknowledges me before men, I will also acknowledge him before my Father in heaven." Recall also these stimulating words of St. James: "If any of you strays from the truth and someone brings him back, he ought to know that he who causes a sinner to be brought back from his misguided way will save his soul from death, and will cover a multitude of sins."

How magnificent could be our influence for good, even in our very limited way! There are souls who do not know all of Christ's truth because of attractive and persistent error, and Jesus speaks of them in this single and wondrous sentence: "I say to you, lift up your eyes and behold that the fields are already white for the harvest." And concerning the sinner, the lost sheep, He says, "I say to you that, even so, there will be joy in heaven over one sinner who repents, more than over ninety-nine just who have no need of repentance." Here is the challenge, and each of us has the plenary power of giving testimony to our Faith, by aiding Jesus in His work of drawing all souls into His kingdom. Christ will not ask for miracles, or for labor which will cause us to neglect our primary duties. He will take care of that, but He waits for our assistance and interest. He wants the work to be one of joint operation.

Mary at Fatima and at Lourdes pleaded for penance and prayer. All Jesus wants of us is that we pray His own will to be done and His intentions to take precedence over our own, that we by good conduct prepare the way for His grace in others' souls, that we live as penitents and be willing to die as criminals with the sentence of death, confident and certain that His resurrection from the dead will mean our own eternal happiness. At the Last Supper Jesus said to His Apostles suddenly, "Amen I say to you, one of you will betray me." Notice how the Apostles reacted. They were men schooled by Christ Himself and about to be ordained as priests by Him. Yet each knew his own potentiality for this greatest of evils, the betrayal of the Son of God. Each asked, "Is it I, Lord?", because it could have been any one of them, and they knew it!

This might be a provocative thought for ourselves. "Is it I, Lord, who so far have done little to assist you?" We might reflect upon the strength of our own faith today or its weakness, upon whether our personal prayer, example and sacrifice have helped any solitary lost sheep to return to the fold, keeping in mind that it is easy to betray Our Lord in His garnering work, if we allow the subtle charm of the spirit of the world to seep into our souls. It would be much better and safer if occasionally we would repeat this question to ourselves, "Is it I, Lord?", than never to think of asking it at all.

Mary is called the "queen of confessors," queen of those undaunted saints of God who on earth prized truth and morality above all improbity and self-love, who knew no aim to living but the design which Christ had planned. In this era when virtue is looked upon as relative, we may have lowered our ideals and lost sight of the high standard of the cross.

We have reason then, to hasten in spirit to Mary at Nazareth, where we shall be brought back to a true recognition of our purpose in life. Mary will repeat for us the opening words of her Magnificat, which she spoke on the occasion of her visit to Elizabeth: "My soul magnifies the Lord." And the Virgin Mother will remind us that we, too, must magnify her Son Jesus, must make Him the cherished object of our own heart first, and then through our manner of life help Him to become the desired of the hearts of others. As "queen of confessors," queen of those intrepid saints of the past who gave their heart without its blood, Mary could instill within us a readiness and a daring to accept the challenge of the Son of God, a willingness to share the Faith, no matter what the cost might be. The criterion of the Master is high, but with Mary it is not too difficult to attain it.

Queen of Virgins

"O HOW BEAUTIFUL IS the chaste generation with glory; for the memory thereof is immortal, because it is known both with God and with men." Looking through the Book of Wisdom in the Old Testament, we find these indelible words, and we are conscious of the fact that, despite the idolatry which the world pays toward flesh, this same world and the devotees who adhere to its vacillating standards are in secret admiration of the power and the majesty which lie inherent in the practice of chastity. These zealots of physique and carnality are in veiled envy of those who walk amid the debris of life, unblemished and unscathed.

"It is known both with God and with men." Yes, God knows well the love which a virgin woman has for Him, her courage and her unselfishness. The Creator looks down upon His virgin and sees that she, within whose frame He placed a cradle for the harboring of life and to whom He gave the awesome power of producing it, has given back to Him the haunting adventure of human love and the fascinating transport which attends it. Men know it, too, when they confront a woman who has kept her virginity in a consecrated way. They know that God has won a vestal heart, a heart that has been drawn to the secret rapture of divine enchantment, rather than to what at best can only be their own pendulous and sometimes faltering affection.

In this life we are all beset with the lure and yearning of the body, some more, some less. These longings lie within our nature because Adam and Eve resisted God's command. Our nature is a fallen one, open to all sorts of temptations. There are libertines who plunge to the very depths in a lifetime search for revelry and satisfaction. Many others, as time goes by, experience unfortunately in legitimate marriage the apostasy of a spouse in the work of procreation. Even unmarried souls at times will exchange their intimacy for the bauble of unwholesome dalliance. Yes, the excitement of the unknown is ever with us, and we have to be on guard with constant vigilance lest the enemy creep up beside us to capture our conscience and integrity. Yet in the face of all this inclination, this hunger for experiment and tantalizing display, there are women in this life who give back to their Creator the body with which He clothed

213

them and the soul which He adorned. They are the ones who can repeat the prayer found in the Book of Ecclesiasticus: "I will give glory to thee, O Lord, O King, and I will praise thee, O God my Savior. I will give glory to thy name, for thou hast been a helper and protector to me, and hast preserved my body from destruction."

Virginity stems from a deep sincere love of Jesus and as a result of His special grace. The virgin soul sees in her Redeemer the One who gave His own Body to be massacred for her. She in turn, desirous of following Him completely and longing to help Him in His work of saving souls, returns to her Master the legitimate use of her own body, with its pleasures and alleviations, its comfort and contentedness. She has the same trials in life as her married sister and sometimes even more, but she remembers the words of Jesus: "It is the spirit that gives life. The flesh profits nothing." All the virgin saints of history, whether they were martyrs or not, loved Christ above all men and, in order to labor for Him more, gave up the ordinary human destiny of marriage. In the liturgy of the Church only women are called virgins, although as we know most of the saints from among men were virgins, too.

All of us are much aware of the struggle to be pure. We are assaulted from every angle. Our media of communication are filled with the seductive rhythm of the sensual. We see it in magazines, in books, on television, and we hear it on radio. We have to be cautious always, lest the spark of desire turn into a flame of restlessness, and then into an inferno which consumes. We have to stay in our mind close to Jesus on the cross. We must reflect frequently upon His passion and His dying, and think too upon the words which St. Paul used to the Galatians: "They who belong to Christ have crucified their flesh with its passions and desires." Each of us wants to "belong to Christ," but it does mean crucifixion. At the same time, however, do not forget the soft and promising words of the Master: "My yoke is easy, and my burden light."

To attain and preserve purity we need the inspiration of Mary who herself is the "queen of virgins." A visit in spirit to her home in Nazareth will be a remedy for the iniquitous desires which assail us. There we shall see a virgin mother whose purity gave her command even over God. And that may be the one fact which she emphasizes. If we sometimes dip into the tainted pond of grossness, we shall feel a stranger to the living God; but if we bravely renounce such indelicacies, stifling the clamor of our flesh, then, although we may find it oppressive and severe at first, we shall find that God is at our beck and call, and we shall discover a love undreamed of formerly. Yes, Mary is the one most effective recourse for those who find it hard to distinguish the dross from the gold. Impurity can make us blind to all the virtues. Mary will strip the shades away.

Queen of All Saints

ALL OF US ARE familiar with death, but it has always been the death of another. We know, of course, that we too must die, and immediately after that be judged by Christ forever. We cannot constantly keep our thoughts on death, for life has been given to us and we must make that life truly fertile. We would not fear death if we were living as God wants us to, but some go along the trail of their own volition, seeking ever the forbidden fruit which God had denied our first parents. These grow old in fear of the imminence of Christ, the Judge. They may lack misgiving now, but the day will come when earth seems barren and they themselves quite filled with trepidation and anxiety.

Only one solid way lies ahead in which to view this gift of life which God breathed into us, and that is to look upon it as the testing ground for immortality in heaven. Here we have the choice of paradise with all its trees, or the one tree upon which hangs forbidden fruit. We cannot afford the luxury of make believe, as if our life here was unending. Our lifetime consumes only a few years among the many centuries which have already gone by, and they will soon be over. In the meantime we have a contract to uphold, to know and love and serve our God. True, there may be failures here and there. Weakness, pride or passion may seem to shackle our free will at times, and we may find ourselves alarmingly broken and remorseful with the impact of reaction. However, we can rise again through the merciful ministrations of the sacraments and face our God, renewed in energy and hope, determined again to go all the way in loving Him.

We were created for sainthood. To live in heaven forever, gaining insight into the Trinity and possessing God, is the destiny of the saint and his reward. To each of us this same prize has been offered. Frequently, then, we should raise this stumbling heart of ours to heaven, realizing that it is the only ambition which must at all costs be fulfilled. St. John in the Book of the Apocalypse relates his celestial vision of the angel with the seal of God who cried out to other angels: "Do not harm the earth or the sea or the trees, till we have sealed the servants of our God on their foreheads." Our moral goodness here on earth will guarantee the impression of that seal in heaven. Again St. John tells of an elder in heaven asking, "These who are clothed in white robes, who are they? and whence have they come?" The reply which St. John quotes is this: "These are they who have come out of the great tribulation, and have washed their robes and made them white in the blood of the Lamb ... They shall neither hunger nor thirst any more ... The Lamb who is in the midst of the throne will shepherd them, and will guide them to the fountains of the waters of life, and God will wipe away every tear from their eyes." These are all the saints of which St. John speaks, all men and women who on earth tried to fasten their hearts upon heaven and their God. Their mortal lives passed quickly, as does our own, and despite life's lamentations, it was thrillingly so worth while.

"God will wipe every tear from their eyes." To us who live in this valley of tears, these are engaging words. We are the sons of Adam, the heirs of original sin, and our life on earth, as we all know, is that of joy one day and sorrow the next. We have dropped many tears along the way of life, some of us more than others. Lost loves and shattered dreams, misunderstandings and confusion, personal weaknesses and loneliness, ingratitude, disappointment and disparagement, all these have caused the tears to flow upon our cheek and in our heart. Yet this is life.

There is no other kind, no matter how diligently we seek it.

In order more clearly to understand that life will ever be this way and how stalwartly we can bear it, we shall journey in spirit to Mary's home at Nazareth, where we shall see a woman who stands poised amid the conflict of impending doom, a woman who, despite adversities which were to break her heart and strip her soul, keeps her face to the sun and her feet firm upon the ground. Mary could not afford to look downward at the distortion and distrust of men. She looked only upward toward the stars beyond which was her Creator who fashioned and predestined her. Otherwise, humanly she might not have stood the strain. "Man," says the Book of Job, "born of a woman, living for a short time, is filled with many miseries." We truly deserve such affliction because of our sins, but Mary was smitten for nothing.

At Nazareth, Mary will inspire us to greater knowledge of her Son and will point to us the way of love without which we can never serve the Christ. She will tell us that the travails of this life which we must suffer are but stepping stones that lead up to the gibbet and the sweetness of the cross. She will quote Jesus and say, "Do not be afraid, little flock, for it has pleased your Father to give you the kingdom." Mary will discuss with us the fear which we have of the cross. From her we shall discover that Calvary in our lives is not an evil, but a blessing, if we can only willingly and generously accept it. We fight so hard against the hammer and the nails when they touch us. Mary will tell us how she stood on Golgotha and was crucified with every thud of the hammer. "Queen of all saints" is Mary, highest, loveliest, most courageous of them all. "God will wipe away every tear from their eyes." That is the promise to us. But Mary will wipe away the first tear that comes from fear of the cross.

Queen Assumed into Heaven

ALL OF US KNOW that our destination is heaven, that we are intended for the sharing of the happiness of God forever. We also realize that in order to reach heaven, we must pass through the strangeness of dying and the mystery of death, for these are the penalties of original sin and of our own personal sins. In the meantime we have to make the very best of life by fulfilling our obligations as adult citizens in the world of men. In our deference to the concerns of men, we must first comply with our obligations to Almighty God by striving always to increase our knowledge and love for Him. That is the way of salvation.

Certainly life becomes difficult at times. We are beset with the basic weaknesses of our own human nature. St. John the Apostle, in his first New Testament letter, reminds us that "all that is in the world is the lust of the flesh, and the lust of the eyes, and the pride of life." These may take their toll upon us, sometimes even dreadfully, for with the violence of a whirlwind they can sweep upon us and obscure our clear vision of God and His heaven. To repulse these onslaughts we must be of high and holy standards, of strong, proper convictions, and habituated to solid principles of morality. Otherwise we may succumb and, for the moment at least, heaven is farther away.

In order to discover pride of life, we may have to peer through endless disguises, but the lure of lust of the flesh is evident to every one. Our image of heaven is blurred when we indulge in lust of the eyes. Our eyes behold on earth the beauty of mammon, things purely material. Here luster and gloss bewitch us, so that we begin to think of the purely physical as an end to be possessed, rather than as a means to a vastly superior end. Articles for bodily comfort and pleasure are manufactured to the saturation point, particularly in our own land. Advertisements appeal to the imagination rather than to sound judgments, and we are inclined to regard ourselves as failures if we are not constantly accumulating these goods. Material wares are designed for better living, but we must be careful lest they contribute to a mode of living so luxurious that we are distracted from God, our last end. Better living most certainly cannot exclude better moral living. Our sense of values is secure when we keep ever alive our goal of heaven.

Because we are liable in some ways to be influenced by wealth and what it can buy, and then come to feel that we can be less dependent on God, we should urgently seek the counsel of our blessed mother who once reigned in her home at Nazareth with little of possessions except the richness of God.

Because the significance of values has been distorted in this modern day and age, we should be wise to journey in spirit to Nazareth to spend a while in the humble abode of Mary. There she would speak to us with gentle eloquence of the spiritual treasures which we may be passing by for the transient harvests of this life. Perhaps she would recall for us from the Book of Proverbs that "riches shall not profit in the day of revenge." From the Book of Ecclesiastes also she would warn us that "where there are great riches, there are many to eat them. And what doth it profit the owner, but that he seeth the riches with his eyes?"

If we would but take time out from our ceaseless pursuit of ownership in life and listen to Mary at Nazareth, she would tell us of the everlasting rapture of heaven. Our blessed mother had so little of what this world offers, and now she has heaven. Is there a necessary connection between the two? No. To have little here is no guarantee of much in the hereafter. It is rather how we regard what we have here that has a necessary connection with what God will give us afterwards. Our sense of values matters, and our heaven is as secure, with the grace of God, as the presence or absence of the desire for heaven in our sense of values.

Queen Conceived Without Original Sin

ALL MEN AND WOMEN are subject to temptation and prone to sin. Some, because of fallacious teaching and restricted knowledge, do things undisturbedly that for others would be wrong. For us as Catholics, however, the chance of error does not enter into the picture. Our Church takes care of that. We know the doctrine of Christ and His moral teaching. In combat against temptation we may find the contest hard, but at least, because we have certainty, the struggle can be a simple one. We have no doubts or wonderings concerning objective truth and morality. Our contention is simply with ourselves. We are caught between two armies, that of Christ and the Church on the one hand, and the divisions of hell on the other. Our life to a great extent consists in forming our mind and deciding on which camp we shall follow. That we want at times to follow both is the trouble. Of course, we wish to be soldiers of Christ, but the discipline of His ranks is sometimes hard unless we have learned how to love Him. Satan has many allies, the flesh and the senses, the sweet breath of the world and our love of self. Sometimes, perhaps, we waver in battle and cross over to the enemy's side, for this is exactly what sin is. Yet, uniquely Christ is a leader who will always welcome us back, at least while the conflict rages, and our life on earth is that conflict. The Book of Ecclesiasticus says, "Never trust thy enemy, for as a brass pot his wickedness resteth . . . Who will pity an enchanter struck by a serpent, or any that come near wild beasts? . . . An enemy speaketh sweetly with his lips, but in his heart he lieth in wait, to throw thee into a pit."

All of us realize our situation and plight. If we loved Jesus completely, giving Him priority in all our loves and dedicating to Him the totality of our being, virtue would be easily acquired. But because we hesitate, because we have a love for something else or an attachment to some other, we do not give Christ our whole heart, and the consequence is sin. We may become mentally obsessed with the idea of illicit fruit, no matter of what nature, and unless we cast the thought itself aside, we are in danger of falling swiftly. In the area of the mind many of our moral battles are antecedently fought. St. Paul declares, "I myself with my mind serve the law of God."

In this contest between virtue and vice which occurs daily in our soul, we would be rather unwise to attempt the struggle alone. We have probably experienced defeat this way before, and it would be salutary for us to seek the help and counsel of Mary who dwells quietly in her home at Nazareth. Let us go there in spirit, fatigued as we are from the weariness of the fray. There we shall rest awhile in the presence of our "queen conceived without original sin." There we shall find rest and surcease from life's dilemmas, there we shall find strength and encouragement to resume on another day the fight for God's glory and our own salvation. Do not think that Mary is ignorant of warfare. God said in the Book of Genesis to Satan, "I will put enmity between you and the woman, between your seed and her seed; he shall crush your head and you shall lie in wait for his heel."

The Virgin Mary was always without sin, but above any creature she understands what sin is and why it is. She has seen its dire consequences in looking with her mother's eyes at Jesus on the cross. Of all the saints she has fathomed best the love of Christ for us, and she discerns the lack of love which we give in return. Because she is so well aware of the reason for our personal sins, we shall hasten to her at Nazareth and imbibe her words. We may be confused at

228

present with the absurdity we show in our own life, the contradictions, the wrong judgments, the indiscreet maneuverings for which we are to blame. Mary would straighten out this disarray for us, and we may be surprised at her moderate and measured solutions. She realizes that we have to live in a world that is both good and bad, and she will not necessarily be drastic in her demands. She thinks primarily of our love for Christ. If that is first on our part and complete, then other loves sought for by our human heart will naturally be subordinate and humble, and that which, perhaps, was formerly dividing us can with God's grace be raised to a wholesome state. Mary might not suggest the scalpel. She might simply prescribe medicine instead.

Mary was conceived without even original sin, and this pristine purity of hers could be a sturdy incentive in all our dealings with God and with creatures. Mary is our queen to whom we owe fealty. We should therefore not be strangers, but seek an audience with her, to speak of our woes and perplexities. Mary, after all, is human, even though she sheltered the divine. She knows our heart is human and subject to both harmony and discord. But out of it all she can produce the masterpiece which will enable us to put Jesus first and creatures second, without the loss of either.

Mary's immaculate conception means that she was

free from every type of sin. She was the purest, of course, among all of God's creatures, but at the same time there was in her no false pride, anger or envy, no intemperance, avarice or sloth. If we ever leave Christ even temporarily for the camp of the enemy, our betrayal stems from one of these capital sins which may be dominating our lives. Maybe we know which one it is; maybe we do not. But this is why we should go in spirit to Mary for a while. She will certainly strengthen our love for Jesus. Then, glistening in the splendor of that increased love, all human loves will have a reflected beauty.

Queen of the Most
Holy Rosary

THE ROSARY SEEMS TO BE just simply a repetition of the prayer, "Hail Mary," while our fingers move gradually along the beads. Tangibly it is just that; yet with countless other millions we know that it is much more. Re-echoing through the centuries, the Rosary is the old refrain to Mary, whose lyrics ever are the same but whose melody is different as it affects each human heart. While the same prayer is constantly repeated by our lips, our mind attempts reflection on the joys and sorrows and glories of Mary's career, as our heart endeavors to check itself from mundane loves in giving its affection to her. To some the joyful aspects of Mary's life are a sufficient incentive for drawing near her. For others the sight of our Virgin Mother suffering is the magnet of attraction. But, for all of us, her glories are a hope that

heaven is not far away and that we shall live there
with her in eternity.

The Rosary is an uncomplicated, modest prayer,
recited every day by untold devotees of Mary. Priests
find it to be a mighty link that binds their thoughts
to her, reminding them that, because she is their
queen, they owe her love and loyalty. The faithful,
distracted as they are by the cares and concerns of
life in the world, find in the Rosary a blessed refuge
to which they may retreat. For every one the Rosary
becomes a harbinger of hope and confidence and consolation. It can become the rainbow after the storm,
the blue sky following the fury of the tempest, the
breath of spring pursuing the blasts of winter.

It is not only the Church that urges us to say the
Rosary. Mary herself has spoken to the human race
directly many times and has warned us that the
Rosary may well be the one effective deterrent
against the madness of the world and possibly eventual ruin. This is why they who have let slip from
their lives love for the Rosary and faithfulness to it
might ponder upon their own paltry and meager con-
tribution to the sanity and safety of their fellow men.
If Mary has herself considered the Rosary so important, then how little regard and esteem have they
honestly for her who seldom recite it at all? How
many minutes of a day does this prayer consume?
Yet how many hours we sometimes waste in the

frivolous, the useless and the futile! Time would not be long in recapturing the glow of real friendship with Mary, were we to take our beads in hand, particularly at a special time each day, and give to our queen the majesty of a few moments' prayer. If we could decide that the Rosary is more consequential than many other affairs, this devotion would soon become a habit, one which would draw down innumerable graces upon us.

Mary has a special mission in this world and it is not an easy task. She must help her Son to gain souls for His kingdom on earth. She wants our help in this assignment, and actually it is the great purpose of our own living. She has no warlike armament to give us in this battle to save our own soul and the souls of others. But she does have the Rosary and, with that extended in her hand, she approaches us and speaks to us the words of St. Paul to the Ephesians: "Put on the armor of God, that you may be able to stand against the wiles of the devil. For our wrestling is not against flesh and blood, but against the Principalities and the Powers, against the world-rulers of this darkness, against the spiritual forces of wickedness on high. Therefore take up the armor of God, that you may be able to resist in the evil day, and stand in all things perfect."

There is scarcely one soul, among the many perhaps who have drifted away from Mary's company, who would ever through malice refuse her the prayer of the Rosary. Most of those who no longer say it, have omitted it for a deeper reason. In their confusion resulting from the conflict within them between the spirit of the world and the spirit of Christ, they have dropped from their lives the spiritual aids which could refresh them. They are lonesome souls, seeking help in fields afar, who have forgotten that true happiness will never be found at a distance beyond which the Rosary can lengthen. Once they veer too far, the link breaks, and Mary becomes but a dim figure in their disturbed lives.

However, there is one consoling fact to remember. If some of us have lost sight of Mary, she has not lost sight of us. She looks at us clearly, for the mist is only before our eyes, and in us she sees souls to love and conquer. If we find ourselves in this position, if we have permitted our attachment for Mary to fade, be brave enough then to journey in spirit to Nazareth where we can recline at her feet and reach out and touch her Rosary.

As "queen of the most holy Rosary," Mary will dispel the haze amid which we may be wandering. If we have the heart of a child she will acquaint us again with the joyful episodes of her life, making it known that finding us would bring her a gladness equal to that when she found the lost Christ Child in the temple. If we are mature adult men and women, she will wisely explain her sorrows, which in some manner we too must bear. If we are both, which we should be, if we have the faith of a child and the heroism of an adult, she will tell us once more of her glory, both on earth and in heaven. She will offer us the Rosary, begging us to hold on to it at every cost, for along its well used path we, too, shall find everlasting glory.

Queen of Peace

THESE FINAL WORDS, written on the evening of the day after Christmas, with the dulcet melodies of this holy season still ringing forth upon the air and with human hearts reconciled in peace both with God and man, bring thoughts naturally and normally of peace and of how we may secure it. The whole theme of Christmastide, and that which could so easily be the motif of all the year, is that of peace—a peace which the world cannot give, a peace which may be had in only one way, the way of Our Lord Jesus Christ. "Peace I leave with you," says He, "my peace I give to you; not as the world gives do I give to you." The last title of Mary in her litany is that of "queen of peace," and if we only but realize it, no true peace can ever be found beyond the reach of Mary's hand. If we ever let ourselves drift outside her pale, then we shall walk again in disorder, where we reach out and grasp the things that perish and ignore the things which are eternal. Mary will remind us of what God once said, as recorded in the Book of Leviticus: "I will establish peace in the land, that you may lie down to rest without anxiety."

Peace and happiness are the natural desire of every human heart and yet our lives are filled so much with restlessness, discouragement and disturbance. We look for happiness and peace among possessions, things that we may have and own, but they cannot enter into the soul. We look for peace in places, forgetting that true peace lies within the heart of man, no matter where his locale may be. We seek peace in the companionship of other people, but men and women fail us because of their own weaknesses and frailties and interests. Only near Jesus and with Him shall we possess a quiet heart, unruffled and untrampled by the agitation of the passing scene.

We have to pay a price for peace of soul. We have to hand over our body to Jesus, our senses, our mind, and our will. We have to surrender, and few of us find capitulation easy. We are so engrossed with love of self, so enamored of the quixotic spirit of the world, so avid for the fulfillment of our own desires, that we find it very much against the grain of human nature to relinquish completely what we have and what we are, to leave these gifts before the throne of Jesus. Strong faith, stout heart and concentrated love we must have, if we are to cede our rights to

237

the Master. Once we can do all of this and do it graciously, the floodgates of heaven will open and the chant of angels will tranquilize our soul, making it content and resigned with either tears or smiles.

Certainly, if we want peace of soul, we must go over toward Nazareth, to the home of Mary who is "queen of peace," and repeat to her the words of Ezechias in the Book of Kings to Isaias: ". . . let peace and truth be in my days." Mary is the one to whom we must go, if we wish to unravel the tangled skein of our lives and finally attain to the placidness of soul, the search for which we spend all our waking hours. She is the one who brought the Prince of Peace to earth and who years later gave Him back to heaven on a cross. Mary is the one who knows best our digressions and meanderings in quest of peace, our futile journeys into night, our feverish pace of the day, and she knows well how empty we are of the very happiness and peace for which we look. She wants us, of course, to stay in spirit some length of time with her, for even she can hardly be expected to accomplish in a day the miracle of converting our heart from its human attachments, its loves and its passions. She will need some time to train us once again, perhaps in honest prayer, and to make us generously willing to mean the words, "Thy will be done." She will need some time before enabling us finally to perceive that nothing in this life beyond her threshold is permanent, realistic or consequential in the end.

So why not make provision for a retreat in spirit from the flurry and the stir of life? All we need take with us to Nazareth is a readiness of will, whereby we have the courage to give up for a short time the things we think we love. We shall go there with an open mind, fain to learn of Mary what she desires us to know. Be gentle with her, considerate and kind. She is earth's most noble lady, daughter of the eternal Father, mother of the Son and spouse of the Holy Spirit. She has reveled in the playground of divinity, yet is as much at home amid the carnivals of men. Go to her with an honest hunger to change and to transform our lives. We shall find before long that many of the things we thought were so essential to our peace and happiness, are not so at all.

St. Paul says to the Romans, "Let us follow after the things that make for peace." Until now we may have been seeking those things only which we mistakenly thought would afford us peace of soul, but which instead brought more conflict and further disillusion. Mary knows precisely the requisite for peace and happiness. It happens to be holiness, which is sincere conformity with the will of God. If we stay with her at Nazareth and do not run away, we shall find, at first slowly but then later at a quickened pace, a peace descend upon our soul, the like of which we have not felt before. It will flood our heart and leave no room for guile, evasion or deceit. We can look Christ in the eye, and Mary, too. Then—who knows?—it may well be that we shall wish never to leave Nazareth and Mary again. If this comes true, then we have made a down payment on heaven!

242

READER'S NOTES